PERISCOPE PATROL

To
Ian Wanklyn

PERISCOPE PATROL

The Saga of the
Malta Force Submarines

John Frayn Turner

Pen & Sword
MARITIME

First published in Great Britain in 1957 by George G. Harrap & Co. Ltd
Reprinted in this format in 2008 by
PEN & SWORD MARITIME
an imprint of
Pen & Sword Books Ltd
47 Church Street
Barnsley
South Yorkshire
S70 2AS

ISBN 978 1 84415 724 2

A CIP catalogue record for this book is
available from the British Library

Printed and bound in Great Britain
by CPI Antony Rowe

Pen & Sword Books Ltd incorporates the Imprints of
Pen & Sword Aviation, Pen & Sword Maritime, Pen & Sword Military,
Wharncliffe Local History, Pen & Sword Select, Pen & Sword Military Classics,
Leo Cooper, Remember When, Seaforth Publishing and Frontline Publishing

For a complete list of Pen & Sword titles please contact
PEN & SWORD BOOKS LIMITED
47 Church Street, Barnsley, South Yorkshire, S70 2AS, England
E-mail: enquiries@pen-and-sword.co.uk
Website: www.pen-and-sword.co.uk

PREFACE

THIS is the story of how a handful of submarines changed the course of the War.

For sixteen momentous months Malta Force Submarines struck out into the unknown from that isolated island—to stop enemy supplies from reaching North Africa. Half of all Axis shipping was sunk; half of our submarines failed to return. . . .

Periscope Patrol picks out the heart-pounding highlights of this underwater war, and sets them against the background of bombed-but-unbowed, magnificent Malta.

J. F. T.

CONTENTS

1

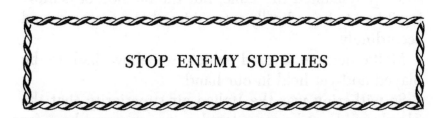

STOP ENEMY SUPPLIES

"Stop all supplies from Italy to Tripoli."

Commander G. W. G. (Shrimp) Simpson fingered the flimsy signal giving him these clear, concise instructions to intercept the enemy's sea traffic in the vital mid-Mediterranean. It was January 10, 1941. Simpson had arrived to take up his duties as Commander (Submarines), Malta, and these orders came from the Commander-in-Chief of the island.

"Not a submarine in sight," Simpson murmured to Geoffrey Tanner, a lieutenant-commander appointed as his staff officer of operations. "Still, I suppose this is as good a time as any. We've just got to start right from scratch. First we'll have to get some subs., then find out which routes the Huns are taking to the North African coast, and then there's the detail of discovering when they can be expected. That's all!" Simpson was speaking as he looked out over Lazaretto Creek, soon to be the headquarters of the Malta Force Submarines.

The war was only sixteen months old, but British policy in the Mediterranean had already suffered a succession of setbacks. The traditional aim was to keep the Mediterranean and the Suez Canal open for the Allies—

and closed to the enemy. When war broke out the British and French fleets seemed strong enough to tackle this task. Then the complete collapse of France and entry of Italy into the war changed the situation suddenly. The strategy remained the same, but the method of achieving it had to be radically reconsidered and forces moved accordingly.

Malta became a card which somehow had to be played and yet held in our hand.

So withering was the Italian air superiority that the island could not be considered as a permanent base for our fleet. But it could become a 'staging post' for convoys through the Mediterranean; and a base for air and submarine assault on the enemy's sea-links with her forces in North Africa. Malta, in fact, was an offensive outpost rather than a defensive base.

Meanwhile the Mediterranean Fleet—safely based on Alexandria—could keep the Central and Eastern Mediterranean free, besides bringing valuable support to the Army of the Nile in its operations along the coastal strip of the Western Desert—with its one road between Tripoli and El Alamein.

This rapidly revised concept of the strategic requirements was justified by the events in the summer of 1940. General Wavell inflicted a thundering defeat upon the Italians; Admiral Cunningham's aggressive policy hit the Italian fleet hard, culminating in the crippling attack in Taranto harbour; and several convoys sailed successfully from one end of the Mediterranean to the other, calling at Malta *en route*.

All available fighter aircraft were tied up in the summer skies over England, but this deplorable lack of air power did not affect the situation as seriously as

later, in 1941 and the spring of '42. The anti-aircraft
defence hammered healthily away as deterrents to the
high-level bombing of the Regia Aeronautica. What
bombers the R.A.F. and Fleet Air Arm did possess con-

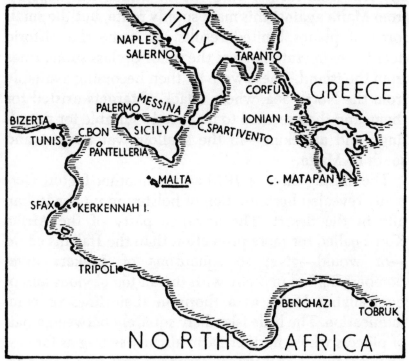

THE CENTRAL MEDITERRANEAN, WHERE 10TH SUBMARINE
FLOTILLA OPERATED

centrated on attacking Italian bases and convoys with
bombs and torpedoes.

With the Alexandria fleet was a flotilla of large 'patrol-
class' submarines. During 1940 one or two of these
would occasionally call at Malta and carry out sorties
from the island. But because of their size they could
only be used in the deeper waters off Italy, whereas it
was gradually realized that the decisive duels would be

fought in the shallower waters of the areas around Cape
Bon, Taranto, Benghazi, and Tripoli.

As the fleet was far away at Alexandria, the enemy
came to concentrate his supplies on Tripoli, to avoid
any risk from farther east. An air attack was kept up
from Malta against this main supply route, but the small
force of planes limited results. So came the historic
decision to operate some of the small U-class submarines
from the island. These were by then becoming available
from the North Sea, where a lack of targets existed for
them, and they seemed to be exactly suitable for patrolling—and attacking—in the shallow waters west and
south of Malta.

The closing days of 1940 added another factor. Germany revealed her intention of bolstering up her Italian
ally in the desert. The advance party of the Afrika
Korps called for more protection than the Italians could
—or would—give; so squadrons of Junkers dive-
bombers landed in Sicily with the all too obvious aim of
neutralizing Malta as a thorn in their lines of communication. The little island lay squarely between a pair
of pincers whose northern arm already swung as far east
as the Balkans and whose southern arm was being re-
forged at Tripoli. They hinged on Sicily. And Malta
stood sixty miles away.

In those distant days air reconnaissance for submarines was an unheard-of luxury. The few planes available for anything but defence were fully occupied in
flying to keep the C.-in-C. constantly notified of the
whereabouts and movements, if any, of the Italian
battle fleet. Information from other sources was meagre
at this stage. Occasionally our Secret Service might send
intelligence of an African-bound convoy, but the only

thing to be done really—once Simpson had some submarines—was to go out and find the enemy and sink
them.

But before the sixteen months' battle began in earnest
he had to establish a base. The area chosen was the
Lazaretto, not far from Malta's Grand Harbour. As if to
underline the urgency of the situation, and to remind
Simpson that this was to be war on land as well as
undersea, Kesselring hurled the Luftwaffe at Malta in a
burst of fierce fury only a few days after the commander's arrival. Three attacks in fourteen days on
Illustrious, lying in the Grand Harbour of Valletta,
marked the start of the siege of Malta. The island went
on the defensive; but the submarines' job was, as always,
to attack: to search and sink.

Nevertheless, the base had to come first. Where was it
to be? The old quarantine station built by the Knights
Hospitallers, on Manoel Island, seemed a likely spot. A
part of the Lazaretto, this had only been used as a
'hotel' for submarines visiting Malta between patrols
from bases farther afield. Now Malta would soon have a
force of her own: Malta Force Submarines, later to be
known as the 10th Submarine Flotilla. And, strangely, it
consisted mainly of 'British U-boats,' the Royal Navy's
U-class submarines.

Overshadowed by the sixteenth-century Fort Manoel
—guarding the entrance to Sliema Harbour, and an
eternal reminder of Malta's stormy story—the Lazaretto buildings sprawled for a quarter of a mile or more
along the southern shore of Manoel, its upper storeys a
warren of passages, stairs, and suites of rooms; below,
long arched-roofed store-rooms on the rock foundations
of the fort; and between these store-rooms courtyards

open to the sky with specks of blue beyond the steep grey walls.

First things first, Simpson said. Bomb-proof shelters were vital, but because of peace-time parsimony none were available. (£300,000 allocated during the 1930's would have been enough.) Now the Navy had to start building them in the midst of a war.

At the back of the store-rooms in the Lazaretto the comforting thirty-foot-deep wall rose sheer. Miners would soon be hewing shelters out of the rock, but the rooms had to be cleared to get to it. The working parties ploughed their way through a miscellany of junk accumulated by the Contraband Control Service in the palmier days of '39 and '40.

Spring-cleaning routed out the rats, who had been living luxuriously in bales of pressed raw cotton as nests —and with several tons of ready-shelled hazel-nuts for food to last years!

Slab and granulated cork, wood-pulp, tons of official records, the skull of a criminal, dozens of drains, and antique fire-extinguishing machinery—these completed the collection. No—one more odd item appeared: tons of ground acorn-husks. These seemed utterly useless. They would not burn for fuel, the pigs turned up their snouts at them, and even starving Maltese goats gave them a disdainful downward glance! But a sailor finds a use for anything. Rumour reported that these husks were a special kind of Yugoslavian acorn used as food for camels, and some genius of the lower deck suggested using these sacks of so-called camel fodder for building blast walls at the entrance to the shelters as they were hewn—the theory being that when a bomb fell outside it might be more comforting to know one would only be

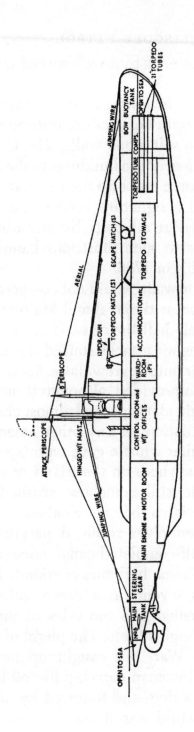

LENGTHWISE SECTION OF A U-CLASS SUBMARINE

B

hit in the back of the neck by a well-stuffed sack instead of a cube of Maltese rock.

In the eyes of the Government the Lazaretto was an ancient monument, with hundreds of historic names and crests carved in the soft stone walls. The Government department handing over the buildings to the Admiralty for the submarine force to set up their operational head-quarters demanded a signature saying that vandalism would be prevented at all costs by any able seamen adding their names to such illustrious handwriting as Emanuel Azzopardi's in 1786!

Unluckily, the Luftwaffe would not co-operate.

The work went on, with naval and Maltese help. The local people had only half their hearts in the job at first —but as soon as the air attacks started the numbers of volunteers and their output grew daily. Soon reasonable protection had been provided, although it meant stand-ing during an air-raid alarm packed almost chest to back without light, ventilation, or any other amenities. And as the already familiar whistle gave warning of a bomb about to burst somewhere on the island or in the har-bours more people still somehow crushed into the shelters—the kennels, as they were called.

The Maltese themselves received permission to go down to the old half-completed canal, once intended to link Valletta and Sliema harbours overland. There they carved out homes seventy feet down, safe from the raids. Rooms tunnelled into the sides of the deep-cut canal. Strange, sad sights these. The plight of people not really part of the War, but caught up in its havoc. People like the old woman carrying her oil-lamp, lead-ing her goats and a dog, and followed by an aroma of the animals. The world was at war.

The draughty discomfort of these early days gradually gave way to cleanliness and comfort. As the submarines arrived amenities appeared, too. Complicated Maltese electrical and plumbing systems were acquired by the Engineering Commander; he also 'found' fans, lights, a cinema projector, refrigerator, machine tools, and the literally legion stores to maintain submarines ready for sea service.

Simpson inspired fresh life into the old battlements and buildings. From being merely an occasional hotel, they slowly took the shape of a ship, as surely as if it were being built on the Clyde: a ship with a soul, with some one to care for it, to alter or adapt it.

2

THE SUBS. GO SOUTH

A TIDELESS sea is the Mediterranean, with clear, deep-blue water, generally smooth in summer but sometimes whipped by the wind into sudden storms of vivid violence. But it is the calmness and clearness of the water which makes the sea so difficult and dangerous for submarines. Their whole purpose and success depends upon approaching a target unseen, yet on a still day the faintest feathery plume from a periscope can be seen for miles even by small enemy ships, and particularly by aircraft. Whatever colour a submarine is painted, its general outline is apparent from an aircraft, even when submerged at quite a depth. And, of course, a sub. cannot stay deep the whole time it is nearing the target. At the outbreak of war Italy had several squadrons of planes specially designed for naval co-operation, and a convoy was seldom encountered without its aerial escort, which could spot the submarines so easily.

Mirage in the Mediterranean is common, too, and played unpleasant tricks at times. Targets would be quite unidentifiable as ships in the early stages of an attack. Weird shapes would heave themselves over the horizon: oblongs, squares, lozenges, and even shimmering castles were watched through the periscope in puzzlement. They grew first in length, then in height; then they vanished—only to reappear as something else. By the time the mass had resolved itself into a respectably shaped ship the submarine commander's eyes would be twice their normal size!

An 'aircraft carrier' off the north coast of Sicily worried one commanding officer for some hours as he gradually got nearer to it. He knew that none of ours were in that unhealthy vicinity—and also that the enemy possessed no such ship. So he started his attack and developed it quite far before realizing at length that the 'carrier' was in fact Cape Milazzo!

As the Italians lived close to the 'Middle Sea,' they knew and appreciated the difficulties it meant for submarine warfare. This might explain the lack of success of the hundred and twenty subs. the Italians were reputed to have had in 1939. The Germans too hated having to operate in the Mediterranean and considered it preferable to hunt in the broad waters of the Atlantic.

Into this southern sea, then, our subs. came straight from the rigours of far-Northern waters. They were about to feel their way for a patrol or two and settle down to hunt, worry, and sink enemy shipping on a scale stupendously out of proportion to their numbers. And the effect on the struggle in North Africa could hardly be conceived: a toll never properly appreciated.

As the basis of the flotilla was being formed its first force amounted to only four craft. They were destined to operate throughout the Central Mediterranean, in an area between Taranto, Sirte, Gabes, Cape Bon, and Naples: a radius of three hundred miles from Malta with occasional sorties still farther off.

This central area, moreover, had its own particular

peculiarities. The submariner likes to dive his craft into deep water and feel unfettered in his movements. In the central zone deep water is only found close to the coast of the southern half of Italy. Stretching southward from Sicily to Pantelleria and Malta is a comparatively shallow sea, while a wide shallow shelf also runs down the Eastern Tunisian coast, bulging out from Sfax to form the deceptive, dangerous Kerkennah Bank, an ultra-shallow stretch, and then eastward along the coast of Tripolitania.

As if shallows were not enough, soundings of less than two hundred fathoms generally meant that mines might have been laid in such waters—especially within the one-hundred-fathom line and close to the coast. And there was a further hazard: certain areas like the large one between Sicily and Pantelleria were declared to have been mined by the enemy on the outbreak of war. Although mines may sometimes be laid deeper than two hundred fathoms, the technical problems involved make it exceptional.

With these widespread shallows and the enemy shipping's strong inclination to cling to the coast as long as they could, Malta Force Submarines were faced with two entirely different sets of hazards—one in the north, the other in the south.

In the north, round the lengthy coasts of Italy, the subs. would be in the enemy's home waters. Here they would meet many large and small bases housing a host of light craft. These would always be in close calling range of an attacked ship. And the enemy's light craft were far too fast for a submarine. It could confidently be anticipated, also, that the enemy would be more alert on his own doorstep—especially where the Italian heel and toe treads—than in the remote 'colonial' coast, farther south, off Africa.

In the southern half of the Malta zone, near the coasts of Tunisia and Tripolitania, the subs. would be working in shallow, mineable waters. Where mines had actually been laid remained complete conjecture, as nowhere south of Pantelleria had been declared mined.

Off the Tunisian coast a submarine's commander had the perpetual headache of how to treat ships found in French territorial waters. It was over-obvious that enemy ships went inside the three-mile limit and even flew French flags. Later on commanders learnt with a satisfied sigh of the action taken by the Government— when the situation had become almost intolerable—in proclaiming that all ships encountered at night south of Kuriat Island were liable to be sunk at sight, and also any unescorted ships during daytime that had given no prior notice of their presence.

Yet another problem presented southward was the low, sandy shore of Tripolitania with its ill-charted regions. As this was an area little used in peace-time, it could not be expected that the charts would be as up to date as those on the busy trade routes. And they weren't! A palm-tree shown as 'conspic' might have acquired several identical neighbours since the map had been drawn; a sand-dune shown as prominent on a chart might have shifted a mile or more, or even have been sunk without trace. And mirage effects could be as confusing as ever. A couple of "large packing cases floating several feet in the air" turned out to be the hangars of an utterly uncharted airfield, while a "pawnbroker's sign" slowly transformed itself into a perfectly peaceful and harmless mosque, with two attendant minarets.

Simpson weighed all these facts and fancies. The convoys would come from Cape Bon, Messina in Sicily, or Taranto. There was no common denominator here. What was certain, then? That they would all have to 'fetch up' in Tripoli. Benghazi was out of the sphere of influence of the Malta subs. The U-class were based on Malta, the T-class at Alexandria, and the S-class at Gibraltar.

Theoretically it seemed easy enough to draw lines between the ports of departure and Tripoli on the chart, stick some coloured pins along these lines to represent submarines, and sit back and await the annihilation of the enemy's supply-ships. But in practice, even if the enemy's route is accurately known, a large coloured pin —however convincing on a chart—far from represents a periscope sticking up a few feet or less in a waste of waters. It can see for a radius of a mere five miles or so, and then only if the weather is good.

To try to find the enemy far out at sea would therefore be futile. And, with the few forces the commander had on hand, it was impossible to keep an adequate watch on the three points of departure in the north. So Simpson was left with the south.

"The obvious place to lie in wait for them seems to be as they're approaching Tripoli," he told Tanner. "More discouraging too, Geoffrey, to have their ships sunk just as they are congratulating themselves on a safe arrival."

So the subs. went south, to cast along the coast of Tripolitania.

3

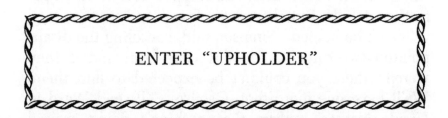

ENTER "UPHOLDER"

SIMPSON stubbed out a half-smoked cigarette and paced the floor of his new headquarters. He awaited word of H.M. Submarine *Upright*. She was on the flotilla's first patrol, north of Tripoli.

"When's she due in, Geoffrey?"

Tanner scanned the sea through his field-glasses. The room's windows were thrown wide. But before he could check the E.T.A. (Estimated Time of Arrival) he saw a familiar slim shape beyond the boom of the harbour through the early morning haze.

"Here she comes," he called, and both men made their way down towards Lazaretto Creek and *Upright*'s berth. They were there long before the sub., and the waiting seemed worse than ever—the sheer suspense of learning the news.

"We'll get a lot of this damned waiting in the next year or two, Starfy." (This was Tanner's title, as staff officer.)

Many anxious eyes followed Eden, the young lieutenant commanding the sub., as he clambered down from the bridge to the perforated metal casing while the vessel secured.

Simpson could not contain himself.

"Well, what luck?"

"Nothing, I'm afraid, sir. Complete and utter blank."

Shrimp Simpson and Tanner exchanged glances, shrugged their shoulders, and stepped over to Eden for further details. But there were few.

"Can't be helped," Simpson said, consoling the disappointed two-ringer. "You did your best, and if they weren't there you couldn't be expected to find them. We'll have one more shot, Geoffrey. I'll send Ward in *Ursula* just to confirm that nothing's doing around there."

A few days later the same scene was enacted with Ward. He found no clue to the enemy's routes to Tripoli.

"Bad luck—eh, sir?" Tanner commiserated. But Simpson did not need any sympathy.

"We've actually achieved quite a lot, Geoffrey. Negative news can be useful, too, and if they're not getting to Tripoli from the north, where we've been trying to trace them, then they're bound to be doing so from some other direction. It's a fair bet now that they think the safest way of staying as far as possible from Malta is to nip across from Trapani to Cape Bon and then coast-crawl all the way south to Tripoli."

Simpson was going to do it by a process of elimination. So Lieutenant A. F. Collett in *Unique* was sent to snoop around westward of Tripoli. It certainly seemed as if the enemy were scared of Malta, although at that time there was little enough based on the island to cause much concern. Until the subs. really found the formula.

Collett was a character. Circular, stocky, and dark, with legs like well-rooted oaks planted to endure. A curly black beard, always trimmed, gave him a fierce expression, which was belied by twinkling eyes. The beard was a flashback to his Huguenot ancestry.

Blessed with boundless enthusiasm, Collett also seemed to have some knowledge of every subject under the sun. Essentially agriculturally minded, he took tremendous interest in the pigs being bred by the flotilla at Malta—known as the Lazarene swine, after Lazaretto! His smart little pony and trap were already becoming a feature in the life of the island.

To while away the inevitable monotonous parts of a patrol, Collett had a hobby uncommon among naval officers: he would take to sea with him a dilapidated tome he had picked up ashore, and proceed to take it to pieces and rebind it.

But on this patrol he had little time to spare, for the first few days went in getting used to strange conditions and lying around on likely sea-lanes. All for nothing. The periscope peered round the horizon ceaselessly. Collett came to check regularly, but found nothing. At night the submarine surfaced to take in air and recharge batteries. The look-out on the bridge by the conning-tower was scanning the sea with his glasses when Collett took over one night.

They were lying several miles off-shore. Almost the moment the commander had adjusted his glasses a light blinked on and off, and bobbed up and down. At last the hunt was on, he thought. Collett drove *Unique* hard on the surface towards the light. It must be a ship. He was sure. The sub. slid on and on until Collett saw some more lights moving swiftly across the night skyline. They passed parallel to the static light. Then the truth flashed on Collett as he got nearer and nearer land. His original light target turned into a house ashore, and the moving lights were the headlamps of Italian cars on the coastal road! *Unique* stayed on the scene for the rest of the night, and Collett made some useful sketches in the last flush of moonlight of objects not shown on the chart. Then she dived at daybreak without having been seen by any patrol craft. *Unique* went east towards Tripoli, and patrolled off the port hoping for better luck.

At last Collett's persistence was rewarded. The silhouettes of the port's buildings came palely into periscope range. He sighted two ships, too. A big one heading for the port, and a smaller sailing out. Collett could not close quickly enough to fire at the first and cursed his luck as he gripped the periscope handles more tightly.

The buildings of Tripoli, standing in the site of a Phœnician city of three thousand years before, faded from view as Collett concentrated on the slow, steady, unsuspecting approach of the second ship. It crossed his mind that she could almost be one of the Phœnician fleet, famed for its daring in the ancient world which was the Mediterranean.

The ship was in the swept channel through the assumed minefield off the port. Her course and speed seemed certain to Collett. He would be firing from such short range that it would be impossible to miss. But the lesson about to be learned was that nothing could be taken for granted when a submarine was submerged. Always there were the incalculables. The state of the sea or the reliability of a torpedo. The weapon itself could certainly get up to some alarming activities, as later actions will show. Anyway, as the stock of torpedoes back at base was only moderate, Collett decided to economize and fire only one. But it missed.

By the time Collett got the sub. round towards the

enemy again the ship had steamed to an acute angle. Her range increased with each second. The chance had passed.

Collett more than made up for this bad luck of being deprived of the distinction of chalking the first victory for the flotilla. This fell to Lieutenant-Commander R. D. Cayley, commanding *Utmost*, who was trying his luck farther westward, near the Tripolitanian-Tunisian border. The date of *Utmost*'s triumph: February 12, 1941. Her victim: an 8000-ton transport. Only a month after Simpson took over.

Cayley commanded *Utmost* from January 31 onward. He carried out attacks in each of the first four patrols and sank four transports totalling 32,000 tons. During the period of sixty days from February 4 to April 1 *Utmost* spent at sea no fewer than forty days altogether —two-thirds of her time—and she was without any defects at the end of it.

Meanwhile, *Upright* varied the search by heading north to the Italian coast. Here she met another hazard of waging war in the Mare Nostrum, when patrolling close inshore near the mountainous coasts. Many of the rivers running down to the Mediterranean become raging torrents in rainy weather, pouring millions of gallons of fresh water into the salty, heavier sea. Depth-keeping for the submarine here could be a positive problem, especially in the final and trickiest stages of the attack—and afterwards. For in the almost inevitable counter-attack it would be fatal for the sub. to have to run her pumps or use high-pressure air to keep a reasonable trim. A noise-source such as this would result in reaction quickly from the escorts of the ship attacked.

Lieutenant J. S. Wraith found this fresh-water hazard

during his famous attack on a floating dock being towed off Cape Spartivento, in Calabria. At noon on this particular day he sighted it with an escort of one destroyer and two torpedo-boats. With great audacity, he dived *Upright* right inside this screen, fired his first tube, and damaged the dock. He saw complete confusion through the periscope. His second torpedo sped to the same spot. The dock went down. Cascades of water crashed over the sea's surface. Wraith retreated rapidly. All went well until *Upright* ran right into one of the patches of fresh water. She sank deeper than any other U-class at that time—340 feet. Wraith stuck out his lower lip.

Up on the surface, the anti-sub. ships picked up the scent and dropped charge upon charge down into the fresh water. The sub.'s bows ploughed on towards the sea-bed. Every one kept calm.

"Level her off quickly, Number One," Wraith ordered.

Daniell, the First Lieutenant, took a step over to the cox'n.

"Can I help?"

Together they wrestled with the hydroplane wheel. Slowly the sub. levelled off.

"Hope we're not diving too deep, cox'n."

Daniell gripped the wheel with all the might he could muster, and muttered: "No requests to revert to General Service will be considered at the moment!"

A grin creased the other man's face as they felt the deck below them begin to right itself.

Water trickled in through a lot of leaks, and the depth-charges kept on coming. Relentlessly. The shell of the sub. scarcely stood the tremendous water-pressure, and shook as the nearest crash flung them both from the wheel.

"Daren't stay deep much longer—and daren't come up far," Wraith said wryly.

Fortunately, the fury of the depth-charging died down as suddenly as it had started, and *Upright* could climb steadily towards the surface and escape.

"Lucky that time, Daniell. Never had a less apt name for a ship than *Upright* while we were floundering in that fresh patch!"

Back to the waters off Africa, and Lieutenant-Commander E. A. Woodward. Here again was the moody Mediterranean.

Woodward drove *Unbeaten* along at periscope depth, trailing a convoy. She moved slowly, for the U-subs. had no great speed or long endurance. But Woodward was just veering into an ideal attacking position, which absorbed his whole attention, when the sub. shook. He gripped the periscope handles—and saw sky, more than there should have been. The craft slithered almost to a stop and struggled to gain ground. Ground, not water, for *Unbeaten* had run slap into a shoal completely uncharted. The sub. lay edging forward at a knot or less, with too much of the periscope and a chunk of conning-tower exposed to the enemy. The water churned itself into a frantic flurry. The nearest escort of the convoy broke off and made a sharp arc towards the shoal. But before she could really head in the *Unbeaten*'s direction the sub. slowly shoved clear and nosed down.

Woodward sighed with relief and ran the slightly off-white sleeve of his thick sweater across his forehead.

"All these blessed charts are a century out of date, I guess."

Unbeaten trailed the convoy once more, after a half-hearted attempt at an attack by the escort, which had broken line to try to reach her. A couple of depth-charges were brushed aside quite easily. All the night and into the following day Woodward followed them. Simpson had discovered the approach route to North Africa by now, so the sub.'s task was a bit better. The enemy remained remarkably unenterprising about their route. For, although it was discovered aboard a captured enemy submarine fairly early in the campaign, and they must have realized that it was known—despite this, the enemy never changed the route throughout the rest of the War.

It made matters a little less hazardous, true; but—as Woodward was to find out next day—there was always the Mediterranean and its fickle bottom. The same convoy hove into view through his periscope. He made all the necessary calculations and dived deep with the intention of surfacing near the supply-ships. Tensely the depth-needle flickered back towards periscope level again. The periscope slid slowly up—and the first thing Woodward saw after the water dripped from it was a destroyer speeding perilously close and drawing closer. Firing was impossible. In a second his mind changed from attack to defence.

"Go deep," he ordered. The sub. dropped down a few fathoms and then touched bottom. They dare not stay there or she might stick. Woodward could not bring her back too near the surface. So, with only eight feet of water under his keel and not much overhead, they lay doggo while the engines of the destroyer pounded and thudded.

The destroyer thought *Unbeaten* was still somewhere near the convoy, even though the periscope had not been seen. A depth-charge shattered the intense silence in the sub., where the slightest sound seemed to echo and even a stifled cough brought frowns from the crew. They were lying in little more than a damp patch. The minutes passed. This was the worst part. The enemy's engines still sounded loud. A stoker was consoling himself with a cup of tea.

"Shut up that noise," came a hoarse whisper across the narrow mess deck. Even the sound of some one stirring tea with a spoon seemed too loud for safety.

In his patrol report Teddy Woodward suggested spoons made of rubber for submarines. But they never seemed to be issued!

In a dozen other patrols Woodward never enjoyed the chances for spectacular sinkings, but he managed to dispose of several schooners around Khoms and a large vessel which was almost certainly a Q-ship. The latter he blew out of the water with a torpedo true on course. These were more than enough to earn him the D.S.O.

A lot of water had flowed through the Strait of Gibraltar since June 10, 1940, when the Mediterranean and its offshoots—the Tyrrhenian, Ionian, Adriatic, and Ægean—entered the arena of conflict and catastrophe. While the opposing armies rolled back and forth across the desert our submarines began to be a positive power influencing the ultimate outcome. Already June 10 and the entry of Italy into the War seemed to have become history: the perilous period when out of the total of four submarines which went on patrol from Malta—only one returned.

Now a new name was to be added to submarine history, that of a Scot who would help to avenge these

C

three submarines sunk the previous year. Malcolm David Wanklyn, lieutenant-commander, was probably the greatest submariner of all time—certainly the first to win the Victoria Cross in this war. And in the sequence of the story he represents the first tangible turning from the defensive to offensive. Wanklyn of the *Upholder*, an apt name for the submarine whose achievements much more than upheld every tradition of the service—it inscribed inspiration afresh for all who followed.

A Scot born in India and educated in England, Wanklyn went from a preparatory school near Haywards Heath, in Sussex, to Dartmouth at the start of 1925. He passed out three and a half years later fifth in his term, gaining the second prize for Science. After the usual service as midshipman he won five first-class certificates in his courses for lieutenant. The merit of the man began to emerge. He started to specialize in submarines in 1932 and first took one past the Rock into the Mediterranean long before the War. In fact, he was serving at Malta when he married Elspeth Kinloch in 1938. Betty came from his own Scotland. The Malta of May 1938 seemed to her far from the hills around her home at Meigle, Perthshire—and, if she could have seen it, so different from the Malta of a mere three years later.

Time was always a relative term, Wanklyn thought, as they gazed out over the still spring night to the Mediterranean. Space too. Malta had the capacity to conjure up the infinite: an island in space and time. Both might go on, yet Malta could stand still, in superb suspense. They crossed to Taormina and saw the Sicilian skyline —tempestuous, triumphant.

From then on Taormina turned into a memory. But Wanklyn was to see it once more—through the periscope of *Upholder*. Three years before, Sicily was a honeymoon setting; now, enemy territory. Intelligence or reconnaissance learned that the Luftwaffe were using one of the big cliff-top hotels as an operational headquarters. This gave birth to an idea which was never put into practice, yet took Wanklyn to Sicily in 1941.

The plan was for *Upholder* to take some Commandos aboard, and, as Wanklyn knew the spot well, for him to navigate the sub. inshore to a convenient peninsula or rock in the bay. As there is no tide in the Mediterranean, the approach would be simplified. A calm night was vital. Then the troops would be landed on the rock, which had vertical sides and a flat top. Once ashore, they were to climb up the high cliffs, blow up the hotel, and return by the same rock to the submarine. So Wanklyn went over towards Taormina, arriving at the depth of night. He surfaced and scanned the coastline. The same hotels which he had last seen in peace-time stood high ahead. The moonlight, streaked over the water, added an air of unreality. All seemed so much at peace. Yet it was war. They could not go back. Not till it was over. Perhaps never.

The plan was checked and timed, then the sub. withdrew to base. So much for the rehearsal. But the operation was never finally authorized.

"Just as well," Crawford commented; "it sounded watertight in theory, but really rather far-fetched." Crawford served with Wanklyn for nearly the whole of 1941 as his first lieutenant.

The two men met at H.M.S. *Dolphin*, Gosport, the Navy's submarine base. But, before this even, Wanklyn was there in 1939. He and his wife took a small house near Havant only a fortnight after their son, Ian, had been born to her in Perthshire.

Wanklyn went down daily to Portsmouth Harbour and across to *Dolphin* in a little duty pinnace. His eyes glistened as the boat chugged and spluttered through the calm water, and he saw several submarines always alongside there, sleek in the sunlight of early morning. He breathed deep the tang of sea air, savouring it as all submariners do.

Wanklyn would soon know only 'night air' while on operations. For throughout the war, of course, the only time a sub. surfaced normally was after dark, in order not to be seen by the enemy. Night was the time for fresh air and recharging batteries. But now it was day-light at *Dolphin*, where Wanklyn's portrait hangs to-day, but where in August 1939 he was an 'additional spare' officer. This did not actually mean that he was regarded as just another submarine service first lieuten-ant, for as far back as 1933 he had been described as "an officer of brilliance."

While war was becoming almost inevitable in August 1939 he joined the *Otway* as Number One. Then he received his first command, always a magic moment. Between January and July 1940, operating from Port-land, he commanded two of the subs. used for special secret assignments, H.31 and H.32.

Then the two men met at *Dolphin*. Wanklyn and Crawford. Commanding officer and first lieutenant. Wanklyn had stood by as *Upholder* was 'building,' but Tubby Crawford joined her down at *Dolphin*.

"What do you think of her?" Wanklyn asked, with almost personal pride.

"She's pretty small, but I suppose she'll be useful where we're going."

Wanklyn looked remote for a moment. "You know, Crawford—it's strange to think that Fort Blockhouse [the alternative name for *Dolphin*] was sited here and came into being because it was out of the way of the rest of the Navy. In the days before the Great War, you remember, they thought the entire notion not cricket at all —and then told the pioneers to come across here to practise their torpedoes quietly. Outcasts, that's what they were."

Now Wanklyn waited to take *Upholder* south to the Mediterranean. This was the moment when he went to war in earnest, this tall and lean man with the soft Scottish voice and biblical beard. The Wanklyn legend was launched.

So *Upholder* followed *Utmost* and claimed a supply-ship on her very first patrol: a vessel of 8000 tons, the same size as the transport despatched by *Utmost*.

Wanklyn's medium hair contrasted with the black beard he was still growing. He brushed his hair out of the way and peered into the periscope intently. The late afternoon of an early spring day. He spotted the supply-ship, then an armed merchant cruiser as escort.

"We'll wait till nightfall, Tubby; then we can surface safely. The range is too great."

Night came. They surfaced. Wanklyn went on to the bridge, checked bearings, and then ordered quietly:

"Fire one." His voice was always calm, never raised. Then: "Fire two."

The seconds slipped by. He looked at the luminous dial of his watch. No bang came from the first torpedo. But with the second the ship blew up before his eyes, lighting the night with a vivid, vehement burst. *Upholder* lay for a second on the surface, exposed by the explosion. Then Wanklyn dived before the escort could counter-attack.

Before steaming back to Malta, Wanklyn encountered another small convoy—and again attacked. Three supply-ships had the protection of a destroyer this time. *Upholder* hit, and probably sank, the central of the three. Then the sub. dropped in double-quick time from periscope depth to within a fathom or two of the bottom. A fifteen-minute spell of depth-charging initiated *Upholder* into undersea warfare as it would be from now on. Imperturbability was the quality which Wanklyn said that submariners needed most. And under this first fire from the enemy destroyer somewhere overhead he felt relieved and glad that no one showed a sign of excitement or unrest.

Wanklyn possessed this quiet quality, needless to say, and added to it two others—resolution and relentlessness. He had an amazing ability of knowing when and where to attack, which soon made *Upholder* the toast of the Lazaretto. Yet the man modestly brushed aside all personal credit for his control of the sub. He said to Crawford: "You know, Tubby—I'd far rather have all this sea to dive into than have to live cooped up in a city just waiting for the bombs to drop." Apparently a submarine did not represent being confined.

Wanklyn possessed phenomenally perceptive powers of navigation. Some people have a 'periscope eye' and others do not. This is an extra, almost intangible quality vital for a master submariner. Or, if not intangible, indefinable. It represents the ability to assimilate all the factors governing each attack—and then hit the target.

One commander back in Britain was a good enough officer, but just could not hit a ship with a torpedo. It was a common failing. But Wanklyn had everything. This was his first patrol. Many more were to follow.

Four further patrols almost without incident gave time for the beard to become longer and more pointed.

Meanwhile, Lieutenant E. D. Norman took over command of *Upright*. He had a hectic week from February 19–26, but at the end of it he qualified for a D.S.O. During the middle watch of the 23rd, when the whole world seemed still, *Upright* spotted a darkened vessel zigzagging towards Tripolitania. Her silhouetted shape suggested that she was carrying petrol. One torpedo from the surfaced sub. sent her to the bottom.

Then on the next night but one Norman again made a sighting while surfaced. The sky was absolutely black when the enemy cruiser darted dimly across the water in the distance. Only twelve minutes after sighting this fast, powerful warship one of Norman's torpedoes struck her squarely and she sank.

Meanwhile *Unique* was undertaking some exasperating exploratory work on a patrol south of the Kerkennah Bank. Collett had the most mortifying experience in *Unique* of making no fewer than twenty-seven sightings of enemy ships without one opportunity to attack: a frustrating fact due to the enemy's being seen at maximum visibility of nearly ten miles. Just the tops of masts and funnels moved across the horizon in Collett's periscope as he swore softly at his luck.

Collett and other commanders were finding that the unfamiliar conditions for attacks attempted at night made success difficult. Prominent among these was the fact that, while surfacing was still necessary before a night-assault could be carried out, the brilliantly bright Mediterranean moonlight, often present, made such a course highly hazardous. In fact, that first victory to Collett on the night of February 11–12 was achieved at full moon. Collett carried it out from a submerged position—a singular success.

4

AIR ASSAULT ON MALTA

WHILE *Upholder, Unique,* and the others in this small band were out on patrol during the first four months of 1941 the Luftwaffe retaliated and bombed the base of Malta—but not the sub. depot itself. These series of sorties lasted from January 8 until May 11. This four months' visit could be regarded as the training ground for the German Air Force in its winter quarters in Sicily. Fortunately for Malta, they would transfer their attention to Russia and the rest of the Eastern Front in the summer; but the raids gave Malta an ominous foretaste of what might be expected to happen the following winter.

And, although this spring assault seemed rather restrained in retrospect when compared to what was to be endured later, the Luftwaffe did succeed in disturbing life in a widespread way. After the attacks on *Illustrious,* lying in the Grand Harbour, the Germans flung dive-bombers against the aerodromes. But these concentrated daylight attacks on the dockyard and airfields proved too expensive; so they switched to night attacks, mingling high-level bombing with low-level minelaying. These intensive parachute-mine operations against the harbours of Malta came as a climax to the 123-day operation.

Simpson pressed the progress of the flotilla's quarters, aiming for safe shelters to accommodate twenty-four officers and 200 ratings—covering his essential requirements for personnel sleeping within the base. The officers' quarters, mess decks, and hospital all came to be located on the first floor, some four minutes' walk from the rock shelters. The buildings had been blessed with really robust walls, but their roofs were vulnerable to blast—and drastically dangerous if they should collapse.

Even though the Lazaretto was lucky in the spring of 1941—as opposed to the following year—Simpson, Tanner, and the rest could not ignore the raids.

Simpson arranged for the subs. not on patrol to lie in a crescent-shaped trot so that a straight stick of bombs could not fall all along it; each submarine was connected to the shore by a floating gangway. This plan seemed sufficient at least while the flotilla did not constitute an objective of the Luftwaffe. When an air-raid alarm sounded the subs. remained on the surface and 'shut off' as for depth-charging. In this way only minor inconvenience was suffered. The submarines in the dockyard for repairs or maintenance, on the other hand, suffered seriously from delays, for the workmen—obeying their orders—retired to rock shelters at the sound of every air-alarm. So at the very time it became vital to hurry work on a sub. to get it out of the target area progress was impeded and the vessel endangered. It was just one of the insolubles of this strange air-and-water war.

The first minelaying came as a bolt from the blue-black-green of the moment before daybreak, when it was a little too light for searchlights to scan the sky effectively—and yet too dark for the planes to be distinguished for interception. They swung inland over St George's, swept round northward, and flew the length of the Grand and Marsamxett Harbours, dropping their lethal loads as they tore out to sea again.

The first mine meandered down, till a crack of ack-ack fire ripped through its parachute and exploded the charge, high over the heads of Valletta's inhabitants. The appalling burst was the first warning the Maltese had of the raid, but they bounced out of their beds and dived into what shelters they could only a second or so before other mines, wafted overland by the morning breeze instead of settling in the harbours, touched down in the crowded area around the 'Underworld' (or shelter area), by the Sliema ferry-landing, and exploded devastatingly.

Over in Lazaretto Simpson and Tanner turned out to see why there had been no warning whistle of falling bombs. The idea of 1500 pounds of H.E. drifting silently overhead was nasty, even though the experts subsequently said that there were twenty-three seconds' grace to get out of the way after they landed.

One or two other officers joined the seniors standing at the end of the veranda. They were all absorbed with watching the efforts to explode the mines in mid-air. Suddenly some one leaned out over the veranda, looked above and behind, and shouted:

"Crippen! There's one right on top of us!"

They disappeared down the dark corridor towards safety, but the one who had given the warning collected a black eye by hurrying headlong into a door half-way along the passage. That eye provoked a welter of wisecracks long afterwards, for the mine came to earth far away from Lazaretto—borne by the breeze!

After that first mining raid never a night passed without its noisy interlude, generally between dinner and about midnight. This meant scant sleep for every one, though it did not matter much to the base personnel. What it meant most to Simpson was the lack of rest for the submarines' crews between patrols. He could still be thankful that the flotilla was fortunate, for no major damage was done in Lazaretto beyond broken windows. The submariners suffered discomfort, yet nothing worse at present—and they collected such useful prizes as the end of a mine casing, which made a splendid pig-swill receptacle, and the aluminium casing of a flare, that became a wardroom ashtray.

The pig-swill was for "Snow-White and the Seven Dwarfs." Wanklyn and more than one of the other submarine commanders sought pacific pursuits as soon as they stepped ashore at Malta, and pig-breeding became a strong favourite. Wanklyn and Collett particularly helped the farming activities. "Snow-White" was an enormous sow, the "Dwarfs" her piglets. Two other litters saw the light of day due to their prolific parents, christened "Mare" and "Nostrum." Despite the bombs and mines—or perhaps because of them—the pigs went on breeding.

The obvious object of the mining raids was to seal the harbours and the environs of their entrances. An excellent system of mine-watching was at once introduced, however, which partially defeated the aim. Nevertheless, navigation did at times become both difficult and dangerous.

The mine-watching method hinged on a heavily sand-bagged observation post, built on an outlying spur of Fort Manoel, where nothing short of a direct hit could dislodge it. Whenever the sirens sounded at night officers manned the post in rotation, and by cross-bearings from other posts really remarkably accurate positions could be plotted of mines falling into the water.

The mines affected surface-ships and submarines alike, yet during the whole of this first four months' onslaught the Luftwaffe did not make a single bombing or mining attempt against the submarines or their base. This was supremely satisfactory from the submariners' point of view—if a little unflattering. For air reconnaissance, which still went on during the day, must have shown the enemy exactly where the submarines lay when in harbour. Yet it did seem strange, as they must have been aware that these few subs. represented the only sea-borne means of offence against the Italy–Africa lines of communication. How heartily the enemy must have later regretted this lack of attention paid to the subs.! For, as events were to prove, they would have saved themselves up to seventy ships if the job had been done, or at least attempted, a year earlier than it was. But now the submarines were still free to carry out their patrols without much interference. Each morning after a minelaying raid the watchers made their report; the positions were plotted with precision; and practically every evening a submarine slipped in or out of harbour.

As a postscript to this period came maps taken from prisoners, which confirmed that as late as April 1941 a particular creek far from the actual sub. base was still shown as "U-boothausen," though any air-reconnaissance pictures must have shown our subs. lying in Lazaretto Creek.

5

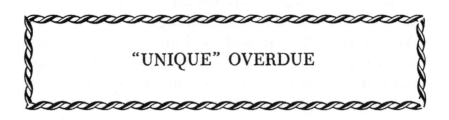

"UNIQUE" OVERDUE

Soon after sunset one evening, with the usual noisy junketings of the previous night past, *Upright* proceeded on patrol. Simpson and Tanner stepped out on the veranda with their field-glasses, as if trying to accompany her as far as they could, shepherding her safely through the minefields. Anxiously they watched as Norman took her slowly beyond the buildings towards the entrance to the creek. Slowly and as silently as possible she edged along. For an acoustic mine would pick up the slightest water-borne sound and particularly disliked diesel-engines.

"So far, so good," Simpson sighed, as he saw her clear of the boom across the harbour mouth. "Pretty tough when they have to keep their fingers crossed to get out of base safely. When you think what's waiting for them in the Med."

"Should be safe now, anyway."

Hardly had Tanner spoken and the two men turned towards the operational offices when a tremor came through the air. They swung round to see a colossal column of water spurting skyward close to starboard of *Upright*. Then came the crack of an underwater explosion, with its reverberating boom echoing down the harbour. They could only watch and wait. The spray spreadeagled and fell in a torrential shower near the surfaced sub. Then the spray settled. But, beyond slight shock at the utter unexpectedness, no damage was done.

"Is she all right?" Tanner asked.

"Seems to be carrying on. What an amazing escape! Must have missed the blast. Might have been sunk before our eyes."

Upright kept to her course serenely.

Norman nosed around Sfax to satisfy himself that the enemy did not lay up there during the daytime, as was thought possible. Then he moved southward to the Kerkennah Bank and waited. He was rewarded early one dark morning by the shape of a small ship, southbound and apparently unescorted. *Upright* moved slowly along the surface, and fired one torpedo, which hit her amidships.

A sheet of flame lit the dawn-dark scene. *Upright* dived desperately, not wishing to be sighted on the surface by a possible escort unobserved in the gloom. But nothing happened. An eerie quiet came over the sub. as she struck a steady six knots down deep. The clear conclusion: a petrol-carrier had been sunk without trace. Norman had evidently discovered a rare route, so he wisely retired to a safe distance and did not return to it for thirty-six hours.

Surfaced once more after dark near the spot where the petrol-ship had been sunk, *Upright* lay with engines stopped, recharging batteries. Suddenly, about 0230, the the officer of the watch on the bridge, "Shaver" Swanston, saw a dark blurred mass three miles away in the port quarter. Straight away Swanston started to manœuvre for an attack. By the time Norman clambered up to the bridge the form had turned into three ships steaming fast in line ahead.

"Right, Shaver—thanks; I'll take over."

It was a perfect pitch-black night. Norman felt sure that a small sub. like *Upright* would not be sighted. It was different with the enemy: they were several strong, and each of them quite a size. He ran *Upright* out, and then whipped her round in a sharp arc, like a puppy chasing its tail, to fire a salvo of four torpedoes at the second—and largest—dim shape.

"Dive."

Norman and Swanston came through the conning-tower almost as one, and dropped to the deck. In seconds the sub. began to submerge. Norman seized the periscope just before it dipped, and saw an eruptive explosion that shuddered and echoed through the tiny craft. Then a second later the flash was washed with the waves, and the eyes went blind.

"What's the depth here?" Norman asked.

"Twenty-five fathoms, sir."

So at 130 feet, with a mere three fathoms below her, *Upright* steadied in her dive and lay with listening gear alerted for anything that might come her way. Sounds suggested that only two vessels were threshing above them—stopping, starting, running round in circles, stopping again and starting. Then the shattering crash of a depth-charge, but none close enough to cause concern. Twelve were counted in the next three hours. And most of the time the chef passed round hot, comforting cocoa, while a sergeant from Lancashire (what was he doing on board?) called "Champion!" inappropriately as each depth-charge disintegrated in violence and vibration.

"When's daybreak to-day, Shaver?" the commander asked, a trace of tiredness mixed with the excitement in his voice.

"About 0525, I reckon, sir. In another quarter of an hour."

Norman watched the minutes tick round till the two hands of his watch were all but overlapping. Then he edged *Upright* gently upward.

"Up periscope."

He could hardly wait to see the scene. A pale, delicate dawn greeted his gaze as he swung the periscope round through its full circle. Just as he rotated it 270 degrees the dull but definite outline of two Italian destroyers came through the lens. They slowly circled the scene, moving restlessly and with disquiet. But before he could close either of them they got up steam and fled at high speed—clearly not fancying the vicinity of a successful submarine attack in broad daylight.

"Can't do anything else now," Norman said sadly, so set course for Malta.

When they got back to base careful interrogation of Norman and Swanston—together with the integration of intelligence reports—showed that *Upright* had sunk no less than an Italian cruiser, the first enemy warship to fall to the Malta Force Submarines. Norman had a shrewd suspicion he had bagged a capital ship, and intelligence plus reconnaissance proved it.

So much for Norman's triumph. But what *was* that Army sergeant doing in a submarine? Living at Lazar- etto were a Special Service Detachment of mixed troops

D

under four officers, whose one ambition seemed to be more and still more excitement. In three months they had seen service from Norway to Malta, and had more action at sea than many fully fledged naval men in years.

They took part in capturing a blockade runner, followed by a brief encounter with the German cruiser *Hipper*, before they entered the Mediterranean. No sooner in it than they saw a spectacular high-level bombing attack on Admiral Somerville's famous Force H, and then they brought their Bren guns to bear in strafing the Stukas and Ju 88's as they swarmed around the burning, battered *Illustrious* before she finally staggered into Malta—with the convoy she and other escorts were protecting absolutely untouched. The Admiral's signal "The convoy must get through" was carried out completely.

These special-service troops embarked in submarines for experience, and certainly found it in U-class craft. They also mounted Bren guns at every vantage point on and around Lazaretto and assiduously manned them during every alert. They hoped to wing a Stuka as the planes hurtled over Valletta like rocketing pheasants after pulling out of their dives on the dockyard.

Later on, the detachment's officer in charge, Lieutenant Taylor, got himself and his section transferred to the Western Desert. Second-in-command, Lieutenant Schofield, was taken prisoner after a successful Sicily enterprise, which no one knew much about at Malta. "Jackie" Broom, who loved high-powered cars but found an aggravating absence of them on the island, and "Sid" Walker, an agricultural expert who advised on the pig production, completed the quartet who led this dramatic detachment.

While *Upright* brought back the sergeant and her crew to Malta, Simpson was pacing his floor at Lazaretto, smoking too many cigarettes and screwing up his eyes through field-glasses as the last light of day died over the harbour. He stayed on all that night at the Signal Station. With the message, sign, or sight he was awaiting still missing, he gripped his glasses again in the faint flush of dawn—searching for the slim outline of a sub. or even a periscope. His eyes had red rims as he turned to accept a cup of cocoa and a sandwich. By sunrise Tanner had joined him.

"Nothing from *Unique*, Geoffrey."

They both knew what this might mean. She was on patrol down south and had been recalled at the proper time, but failed to arrive. So much short of disaster could have happened to prevent her keeping a rendezvous arranged or returning home to time that no real anxiety was felt for the first twenty-four hours. But doubts began to arise then. After another day there would be a mounting momentum of concern.

"How long is it now, sir?"

"More than thirty-six hours."

Simpson turned to the signals officer:

"*Upholder's* returning to base. Will you warn her that she might meet *Unique*?"

Little else could be done. That was the maddening, nerve-racking part of it all. Fears for *Unique's* safety were rising rapidly now.

The first forty-eight hours had passed.

Simpson left the signal station during the day to attend to the rest of the flotilla. Then he returned to it to face another night. Suddenly the signals officer handed him the copy of a message.

"Just received this SOS, sir. It was picked up by Malta W.T. station from the Italian ship *Fenice*."

Simpson snatched it. A glance at the position given told him that the ship lay on the route *Unique* had used to proceed to her patrol area.

The commander was delighted at this shred of evidence, and phoned Tanner.

"Geoffrey? Thought you'd want to know that there's a chance for Collett. We've had an SOS from some ship on *Unique*'s route out. At least there's a spark of hope."

No other sub. was within miles of this spot, so it seemed feasible that *Unique* might have broken down with her radio out of action. Simpson got some sleep back at his office. Next morning his phone woke him.

"Commander Simpson, sir? Signal Station here. *Unique*'s in sight, sir."

Simpson rushed over to his door and on to the veranda to make sure with his own eyes. There she was, slowly coming in. He met her at the berth. Collett emerged, smiling broadly at having opened his score.

"We were worried," Simpson said in understatement.

"Me too, sir," Collett grinned. "I began to think I'd never get recalled."

"But what about our signal telling you to return?"

"Haven't had one, sir."

By some misunderstanding the recall signal was either never transmitted or never received. Collett was getting a bit restive at being tethered so long in an arid area, and just contemplating taking the law into his own hands when *Unique* intercepted the signal from base to *Upholder* about the sub.'s delay. Apparently they're expecting us back, he thought, so we'd better go. It was just after dawn on the next day, when *Unique* was already on her way home, that she sighted three escorted ships in convoy. Rejoicing at his luck, Collett went straight in to attack the largest; but this zigzagged away, leaving him to be content with the second best— the unfortunate *Fenice*, whose distress signals Malta had heard.

"A happy ending, anyway," said Simpson. "Well done, Collett. And we'll try to be more careful about those recalls in future."

6

THE spring came and went, and with the warmer weather the Luftwaffe's attacks began to cool. It looked like transferring to its summer quarters on the Eastern Front at any time. In fact, the raids stopped altogether by May 11. With the better weather, too, came more comfort in the Lazaretto quarters. The sun shone strongly, casting deep shadows into the dramatically arched openings of its buildings, and Malta assumed an exciting black-and-white character of contrasts. Life became bearable again.

Reinforcements arrived to encourage the flotilla and enable it to put out more and more patrols. And, as the enemy's routes were by now well known—and his idiosyncrasies studied in detail—Shrimp Simpson had enough submarines to open up new areas. So they started to work slowly northward.

Yet another arrival to send a shiver of enthusiasm through the shore-based men of Malta was a quartet of destroyers. Up till then the island's defence consisted of a few Wellington bombers, fewer still Swordfish of the Fleet Air Arm, and Simpson's subs. When there were enough numbers to make an attack worth-while the

Wellingtons strafed enemy ports. The more economical assault on his sea-borne traffic when his supplies were concentrated in ships and not dispersed before loading or after unloading could only be carried out by the Swordfish and submarines.

Splendid as the Swordfish were, however, they could only carry one torpedo at a time, which necessitated an immediate return after every attack. The submarines succeeded better, carrying more stings; but they in turn were handicapped by lack of speed: this frequently stopped a second shot at a convoy if the first missed. Often, moreover, they just could not catch a convoy at all. Despite this, the subs. were scoring at a phenomenal pace, which went on for the next twelve months.

No sooner had the low line of sleek destroyers arrived and refuelled than their first call came. They ploughed out of port full of enthusiasm, but their first two sorties were uneventful—except for an incident illustrating Wanklyn's original and decisive forethought. He was always on the offensive in *Upholder*, regardless of the circumstances, even when an opportunity scarcely seemed to exist.

Upholder had spent all her torpedoes on this particular patrol, and was returning off Kerkennah when the destroyers set out from Malta. So she was given a route well to the north of their line of advance, and advised what was afoot. It was at this stage that Wanklyn sighted an enemy convoy. He also knew that enemy air reconnaissance happened to be pretty liberal just then. The odds were that the destroyers would be spotted from the air crashing off to the south-west. Assuming this would be so, the planes would report the presence of destroyers to the convoy by radio, whereupon the convoy would return northward to await a more favourable chance.

Wanklyn was thinking aloud: "How can we intercept the convoy, Tubby, and make it change its mind so it will fall into the arms of our four friends? I know. We'll surface and try to deflect it!"

As he had no torpedo left, Wanklyn ordered some star-shell to be fused and made ready. Then *Upholder* hung around off the romantic island of Pantelleria waiting for nightfall.

Just as he had reckoned, along came the convoy, Sicily-bound. Wanklyn got nicely ahead of it, surfaced, and made a brave show with his absurd little 12-pounder gun, firing off star-shell over the bewildered convoy.

"Looks like a Brock's Benefit!" Wanklyn shouted, his eyes gleaming in the light of the shells.

The stars scattered firework-fashion all among the enemy—and the miracle happened. Almost at once the enemy turned and once more sped off southward, feeling, no doubt, that it would be better to risk the reasonable chance of arriving more or less intact at Tripoli than the destruction that apparently awaited them in these eerily lit waters. As it happened, they were lucky. For despite the star-shells being seen by the destroyers, the warships were unable to make up for lost time, and the convoy arrived whole.

The destroyers had their revenge a few days later, when they caught and destroyed an entire convoy after dark off the notorious No. 4 Buoy at the eastern end of the Kerkennah Bank—which was littered with wrecks from then onward.

On his next patrol Wanklyn was sent to finish off a destroyer which looked salvable if found by the enemy.

He could not get close enough, though, so took *Up-holder* alongside a stranded German ship, *Arta*, in dazzling daylight to see what he could do with it. The boarding-party scrambled up the sides of the enemy vessel and heaved themselves on to its deck. Here they had to tread over bodies, trucks, and motor-cycles. The equipment was all intended for the desert war, but would never get there now. They went below to the captain's cabin to search for papers, but in trying to blow open its obstinate safe they set the ship ablaze sooner than they had planned. Flames crackled across the cabin and spread through the rest of the ship. They retreated rapidly, stopping only to collect a Nazi flag, a few tommy-guns, and other souvenirs before stepping smartly back aboard *Upholder*. The sub. moved off quickly and dived. Wanklyn saw the ship in flames through the periscope. Not till its upper deck was drenched by the Mediterranean did they die down and the ship sink.

On her sixth patrol *Upholder* sighted a convoy of five supply-ships strongly escorted by four destroyers. Such an escort indicated that the ships must have been more than normally valuable. Wanklyn went into the attack, torpedoed the 7000-ton supply-ship *Bainsizza* and the slightly smaller German vessel, of the Fels Line. Both sank. Then he damaged the third supply-ship, about the same size as the *Bainsizza*. One of the destroyers stayed behind as escort to the damaged ship, while the other two sped for safety from the unseen eye. Later the same day Wanklyn closed in and sank the damaged ship. In one convoy he had scored three successes.

About this time Wanklyn won the D.S.O.—"for skill and enterprise in successful submarine patrols." His

Number One, Tubby Crawford—or, more formally, Lieutenant Michael Lindsay Coulton Crawford—was awarded the D.S.C. Others in the crew were recognized too.

So the score mounted monthly. *Unique, Utmost,* and *Ursula* had all broken their ducks. *Upright* had sunk a petrol-carrier and a cruiser. *Upholder's* story had started to take shape. The whole flotilla was on its toes when Tomkinson arrived.

7

FOUR TORPEDOES—FOUR HITS

"Tommo" turned up in *Urge*. He had already opened his attack before entering the Mediterranean by sinking a fully laden 10,000-ton German tanker on his way out.

A great man was Tomkinson, in every way. There have been many tall submariners, but his six feet four inches was well above the average of even the taller commanders. And when he went below he looked like a giant groping into a toy ship. For the U-class ships were all small.

Characteristically, like a batsman looking for runs, he got off to a stupendous start in his first patrol from Malta with a determined onslaught that put down half a convoy of four. Foraging between Lampedusa and Pantelleria, a hitherto unexplored area, *Urge* sighted a south-bound cruiser force screened by destroyers. Clearly the Italians by now appreciated the potentialities of Malta's four new-found destroyers, and were forced to give greater protection to their convoys. The enemy were still a long way off, but Tomkinson continued to close at his best speed. The tell-tale feather from his periscope was picked out from several thousand feet up by an enemy aircraft reconnoitring ahead of the cruiser force.

"Hundred feet," Tommo ordered. For a while the sub. continued its course blind, and then Tomkinson decided he had been below long enough.

"Periscope depth."

The instrument broke surface as slowly as could be managed, so that they should not be seen. Tomkinson took a rapid look round—and found that *Urge* lay right ahead of the largest and most heavily protected convoy met so far by the flotilla, two medium transports and two tankers escorted by five destroyers. Here were the four ships of the convoy he was to attack, plus five fierce escorts.

Tommo manœuvred *Urge* undetected between the screening destroyers and the targets. And at short range he fired four torpedoes. Not one missed.

A tanker and a transport were each hit twice. A colossal combined bang jerked the men in *Urge's* torpedo compartment off their feet. They were rattled like peas in a can. The counter-attack began, at a frightening intensity, but suddenly stopped short: a sure sign that survivors were being rescued from the sunken ships. They could not risk depth-charging in a sea full of Germans. *Urge* therefore withdrew discreetly, to reload her tubes for another day.

One of the *Urge's* men, whose job was tending auxiliary machinery in an isolated tiny compartment, had been a steeplejack before joining the Navy; like his commander, he was exceptionally tall. No one knows what he felt like, cramped in that confined space while the torpedoes exploded and then the depth-charges crumped close by him. Perhaps he longed for the lofty heights he had known, with their comparative safety of peace and a pension!

The torpedo tubes were not loaded in vain, for next day Tommo found the cruiser force he had mislaid when compelled to dive to escape the reconnaissance plane. This time no plane was present. He managed to intercept the force at medium range and risked all on a single salvo. This was not a force to be trifled with, so he attacked as quickly as he could. The dispersed salvo of four cut through the water towards the cruisers returning northward at speed. They missed the cruisers—but the sternmost two caught an escorting destroyer and sank her!

"Dive deep," Tommo ordered, almost before the bang. He took a last look at the destroyer dipping at the bow as *Urge* submerged. Both attacker and attacked were below—but only *Urge* would be surfacing again.

Urge's crew had faith in Tomkinson, as strong as the *Upholder*'s men had in Wanklyn. Despite being a rigid disciplinarian, he would fight against anything he considered detrimental to the comfort of his company. He was devoted to the idea of a happy band of men bound together for a purpose. He used to talk to Tanner of a small family coal-mine he hoped to manage one day. Every one in subs. had to be a bit fatalistic; but they also kept a spark somewhere, an image of what they would do after the War. Something to strive for, to keep them going.

"You know, Geoffrey, old fellow," he would say, "I'll try and run that little mine like a ship."

He personally knew the value of interest in a project and loyalty from all sides. And as Tanner listened to Tommo's plans he thought there would be no happier or harder-working miners anywhere. The only shadow stabbing the picture was whether Tommo would survive to see the War won. If ability meant anything he ought to. For he brought a new definition to 'daring.' He was no spur-of-the-moment man. He summed up a situation —at speed—and went into things with his eyes open wide, knowing what he was going to do, how it would be done, and aware of all the risks.

Despite the disciplinarian in him, he had a wonderful feeling for fun, whatever the conditions. Anyone accompanying Tommo could expect anything. 'Tug' Wilson, for instance, went to sea in *Urge* for some fun and games —and got them. He was a short, dark-haired, round-eyed man, with a flashing smile and a bouncing personality. He was only visiting the flotilla on other business, but the patrol was thrown in for good measure. One evening, several days out, with the bread less than fresh and the vegetables distinctly flabby, the small group of officers sat down to a meal in the wardroom— a couple of fathoms beneath the waves of the Mediterranean. Before anything appeared on the table along came the cox'n to dish out some large white pills: two apiece all round.

"What on earth are these?" queried Tug, looking at the pair of pills rolling round his side plate.

"Oh, some vitamin tablets or other," said Tommo, solemn as an owl.

"What's the idea, though?"

"Well, you see, old boy, after a few days out on patrol, what with the stuffy atmosphere, the victuals tailing off, and one thing and another, the medico tells us to take a couple of these 'buck-you-ups' every day to keep up to scratch. Down she goes!" said Tommo, going through the motions of swallowing the pills, but actually keeping them in his clenched hand. The other officers followed his lead religiously—except that Tug took his pills like a good boy. Needless to say, the 'vitamin pills' were in fact the very latest concentrated Admiralty Pattern No. 9! No need to dwell on the subsequent difficulties of poor old Tug in a small submarine on patrol! The fun and games got into their stride with the enemy soon afterwards, but Tug had little enough enjoyment.

Only by outlets such as these could anyone keep sane, going out week after week, month after month. Until what? "Fifteen patrols and then home" was the general rule. But exceptions existed. They might do more—or less. The sub. might be lost or extensions could be granted. Meanwhile Tomkinson recorded the first torpedo hits of the War on an Italian battleship. And the gradual northward drift developed to hunt around the Strait of Messina. *Upholder* spent a short reconnaissance patrol in the southern approaches without finding much to report. Then Wanklyn went into Malta to take his place for one of the two most outstanding actions of his career—to be recognized by the Victoria Cross.

8

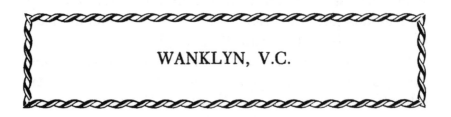

WANKLYN, V.C.

WHICH was Wanklyn's most perfect patrol? Students of submarine strategy might argue for ever, just as they could compare Wanklyn with Tomkinson. When two giants serve in the same flotilla such discussion is inevitable. Between their efficiency and success as sub. commanding officers it would be hard to choose. They had something else in common too, as their later experiences will show.

Tall and thin, with a nose straight from a Cruikshank cartoon character, large, flexible, powerful hands, and the pointed, yet a little ragged beard—that was David Wanklyn, a friendly, fierce figure, who could not help catching the eye. His own eyes would on occasion blaze brilliantly with an intensity of purpose and dedication. Or they could crinkle and laugh, for he was a soft, gentle soul, too—one who hated to think of the consequences of his actions after a ship had been hit.

Returning from patrol, his eyes would be red-rimmed with the strain of days and days with not enough sleep —and an endless responsibility, one which went on even while he was snatching hours off duty. And, with his electric eyes set in a bearded face, David Wanklyn conveyed the inevitable impression of one of the fervid revivalist preachers who stormed through the country in the nineteenth century. The resemblance did not end there, for Wanklyn had some indefinable power which drew the very best from men.

Shrimp Simpson—also an enlightened leader—wrote of Wanklyn about this time that his "exceptionally fine character made him a natural leader who received automatically the loyalty and maximum effort from all who served with him. As an example of this, two or three worthless scamps have been drafted to *Upholder*, never again to appear at the defaulter's table." Which was one extremely efficient way of dealing with a luxury that could not be afforded at Malta in 1941—a man who would not pull his weight.

So, under the command of a man whose appearance and style seemed more in keeping with the sixteenth century than the twentieth, *Upholder* flew her flag—the Jolly Roger—with as ardent a spirit of adventure enshrined as an Elizabethan galleon.

So to the seventh patrol. The little sub. set off from the narrows of Lazaretto Creek, watched by the faithful Simpson and Tanner. A pencil-slim shape with thirty-odd lives linked to her. Almost at once they went to 'diving stations.' At the order all on the bridge except Wanklyn with one signalman clambered down the ladder of the conning-tower. That would be their last look at daylight for many days. From then on they were cooped up in a steel shell about the same cross-section as a London tube-train.

The diesel engines were at 'full ahead,' and the boat pitched in the swell, as she was still on the surface. At this stage all was orderly confusion. Various shouted

E

orders sounded from forward and aft. Then suddenly
above the din came the hoot of the diving klaxon at its
piercing pitch. Silence as the diesels coughed and spluttered to a stop. Then at once the regular quiet hum of
the electric motors. Number One was speaking sharp
routine orders in a level voice as Wanks' legs appeared
on the ladder into the control-room. The hatch slammed
shut above him, and he slid his body down to the deck.
They were in. The needle in the depth-gauge swung
slowly round to ten, fifteen, twenty, twenty-five feet.
The water was above them now.

Number One went on with his orders for a 'trim' dive
as soon as they were out of the harbour, to see that the
balance was still all right after taking on provisions.
They did this in the narrow search channel, the area
already swept for any possible enemy mines.

"Pump on A . . . stop the pump. Flood Z . . . shut Z."
And as the needles of the depth-gauges passed twenty
feet deep *Upholder* lost the effect of the surface swell.
She stopped creaking and settled down to a steady
underwater course. The silence came as swiftly as the
change-over from diesels to electric motors.

As it was daylight when she did her trim dive, she
stayed down at about fifty feet and surfaced about
three-quarters of an hour after sunset. All was quiet.
This enabled batteries to be charged and fresh air to be
renewed. She switched over to diesels for the night and
proceeded along the surface at about six knots. Any
higher speed coupled to her wake would have made her
visible from the air or even to other ships. Once in the
patrol area, the speed was normally raised to eight–ten
knots, for the faster the sub. was travelling the faster
she could dive. The notorious Mediterranean phos-

phorescence was also present, and Crawford could see it through the periscope. It could be so strong sometimes that it showed up the whole form of the sub. to aircraft or ships.

The crew split into watches: two hours on, four hours off. The routine started: sleep—eat—duty—sleep—eat. The only difference between day and night was that during the daytime *Upholder* ran submerged and clear of the effect of waves, while when night came she had surfaced, and rolled and pitched to the sea. And, with the conning-tower hatch open, smoking was allowed. The amount of sleep possible to put in was amazing, due largely to the lack of oxygen when submerged. Towards the end of the day if a match were struck it just flickered and faded. Exercise did not exist, and the men moved only a few paces in twenty-four hours. They were always tired—and hungry.

On this patrol *Upholder* headed for the southern approaches to the Strait of Messina—between Sicily and Italy—still fairly new ground, where detailed information of any kind was lacking.

The beginning was bad on this particular patrol. Less than a day after leaving harbour Number One came up to Wanklyn.

"One of the torpedoes in the tubes has developed an air-leak, sir—it'll have to be changed."

Space in a submarine is limited—in a small one like *Upholder* doubly so. The crew lived up in the fore ends. And the torpedo compartment was only a few inches longer than the torpedoes themselves. As they set out this compartment housed four torpedoes, two in each side as reloads after firing the four in the tubes. Space in between these reload torpedoes was cramped.

To haul the offending weapon free from its tube into this compartment already containing four more torpedoes, and then to shuffle them around to be able to load one of the spares into the empty tube, would have been quite a manœuvre even in harbour.

At sea, under patrol conditions, it became an onerous operation. But it was done, at half-past four on the afternoon after leaving Malta. The crew were wiping sweaty foreheads till a long time later. Normally, of course, the torpedo in the tube has been fired, and reloading is by comparison quite straightforward.

During the first four days after entering the patrol area three separate groups of coast-hugging vessels were the only sightings made, but their size was not sufficient to justify *Upholder* publicizing her presence.

On the evening of the fourth day, though, the long games of piquet, which had passed the tedium, suddenly stopped for the rest of the patrol. In one corner of the cramped control-room an operator was rotating a dial and listening out for enemy ships. For sound travels a long way under water. He concentrated on one bearing, then rapped out a report:

"Ships bearing red two oh, sir."

Wanklyn stepped over and motioned with the palms of his hands for Tubby Crawford to take her up to periscope depth. Crawford then took over the trim. The navigating officer prepared to do the plot. The torpedo officer took over the 'fruit machine' for calculating the relative positions of ships and sub.

A sharp order or two from Crawford, and the boat rose steadily. When it was nearly up to the depth at which the top lens of the extended periscope would break surface Wanklyn said in a level tone:

"Up periscope."

One man was already on the periscope lever, so that as soon as he heard the order he could carry it out. A slight swishing sound, and the periscope shot upward. Wanklyn was ready for it and bent double to meet the eye-pieces as they rose between his feet. He straightened to a standing position with his eyes glued to them and his hands grasping the handles on either side. A flick of his fingers and the periscope stopped dead with its top lens just out of the water. The foam fell from the glass, and Wanklyn took a quick look around the sky for any aircraft; then he scanned the surface.

He concentrated on the bearing given—red 20—and breathed out quietly as smoke on the horizon gave away the presence of a convoy of one escort, two tankers, and a supply-ship. They were a long way off. But, even so, he did not risk the trail of the periscope a second longer than necessary.

"Down periscope . . . fifty feet."

This might be something exciting or just a minor engagement. Who could tell? His hand reached for the buzzer.

Action Stations sounded.

Movements were fast, though there was neither noise nor scramble. Hammocks swung. Many had been asleep, but no one yawned. *Upholder* put on full speed. Time for another check, so Wanklyn nodded to Crawford again. The sub. planed up. She rose steadily. A glance to the periscope operator—and the lanky Wanklyn was uncoiling himself as the instrument came up.

Despite full speed, he could not close to less than three and a half miles. He went on rapping out the details. Course, speed, bearing, range. A chap read off the bearing indicator, port or starboard, and worked out the range. Finally the torpedo officer set various dials on the large box attached to the bulkhead. Then, with the complete picture, he pulled a handle at the side —and the 'fruit-machine' co-ordinated all the settings to produce the one vital 'torpedo firing angle.' This is the aim-off necessary to allow for the time the torpedo takes to reach a moving target.

Wanklyn took her up once more to see that the ships were still on the same course and the sub. roughly where he wanted her. Then:

"Down periscope . . . one hundred feet."

At the precise time he calculated Wanklyn gave the sign, and the depth-needle swung back to 80, 70, 60, 50. Things were tense. Now he fell almost flat on his stomach. No time to swing round the horizon. Anyway, the periscope was set at the firing angle. He waited for the target to come into the lens. But by now the ships were almost invisible against the land—and nearly past *Upholder* altogether. The horizon stayed dark and empty for a few seconds. Then a 4000-ton tanker's bow came into the sights. It crept across the lens. Passed the centre wire of the periscope.

"Stand by . . . fire."

Wanklyn fired his first salvo of four torpedoes; but the cap of one tube failed to open, so only three torpedoes left. A series of slight jolts of recoil as they left the tubes. Then the next order quickly.

"Down periscope. Go deep."

The depth-needle fairly raced round the dial—far quicker than it came up from the one-hundred-foot mark. Wanklyn had his eyes glued to his watch. From the range—far more than normal—he could calculate to the second how long it would be before the torpedoes would cross the enemy's track. His nails bit hard into his hands as the tiny little second-hand made a complete revolution and then another. Only ten more seconds to go. Two more . . . one . . . none . . . silence. . . . Then the musical metallic ping of impact of torpedo against hull, followed by the rumbling, thunderous explosion.

"Nice work, sir," Crawford whispered.

"Only one," Wanklyn said.

Then the two others exploded on the shore beyond. They knew these could not have been hits on ships, as the range was wrong. Wanklyn had estimated the distance to the shore—four and a half miles. The extra seconds' delay accounted for the mile farther the torpedoes had travelled.

But long before the ship was hit or the torpedoes banged on the beach *Upholder* had dived. For from now on she became the hunted—not the hunter. Silence was imperative. A spanner dropped could be disastrous if it were heard over the enemy escort's hydrophones.

The first depth-charge went off. Two, three—the petty officer telegraphist counted them and jotted them down in his log as casually as if he were writing his diary of a day in the country.

Closer and closer the noise came. Intelligence had discovered that their charges were being set to go off at depths of 50, 100, and 180 feet. So Wanklyn chose:

"One hundred and forty feet." He had altered course 120 degrees from the firing position. For 180 degrees, the direct route away from the target, would be on the torpedo track, which could be traced.

Three more charges exploded. The sub. shook. The

noise was deafening. That was all. *Upholder* retired southward to reload her tubes.

Three days later Tanner got the terse statement back at base:

"Asdic and hydrophones out of action."

This meant that *Upholder* was deaf when submerged, without her ears. She would be deaf in the sense that near-by noises would still be altogether too audible, but the whispered sounds in the distance, which give the sub. timely warning of enemy movements overhead and of impending counter-attack, would be totally unheard. Any noise heard by the naked ear continued to be too close for comfort—especially a destroyer's propellers.

Wanklyn was sure he knew the route the enemy used southward from Sicily and, sure enough, on the third day after the engagement with the first convoy, May 23—in almost the same spot as before—he sighted a second convoy of two tankers and an escort vessel. The enemy armies in Libya must have been anxious for its petrol if the navy were prepared to send two more tankers through the identical location of a successful submarine attack only seventy-two hours earlier.

Wanklyn went to periscope depth to take a look.

"This is going to be a pretty problem, Tubby," he said, still peering into the periscope. "The blessed escort is turning back northward now that they're through the Strait."

It seemed strange to be leaving a couple of tankers to the mercy of the Mediterranean just beyond Messina if they were bound for Libya.

"I wonder if they're really going across, Tubby. The names and colours on the ships' sides are confusing, to say the least. You take a look."

Crawford saw colours that appeared to be French. But French and Italian tricolours looked very much alike when viewed through a periscope at long range. Even if they were French, though, their course and present position seemed strong circumstantial evidence that the ships were being employed by the enemy.

One ship was distinctly named *Alberta*, while the other looked like *Damiani*. Wanklyn thumbed his way through nautical reference books, as he wanted to be sure of his ground—and time was getting short. Not the best moment to balance legal niceties, when trying to position a submarine for a tricky attack. Neither of the two main shipping-lists gave a French *Alberta*, but Wanklyn suddenly saw the name.

"All right, Tubby—she's Italian. Or, at least, there's one of that name and nationality. But I still can't find *Damiani* at all."

"Going ahead, then, sir?"

Wanklyn had thirty seconds to make up his mind. To fire or not. He looked once more. The ships looked both heavily laden; they steered a southerly course; and both their names bore a striking Italian flavour.

"They're up to no good—we'll attack."

He fired three torpedoes. They shuddered out of their tubes. One of them hit the *Damiani*. She started to settle by the stern. *Alberta* began a series of convolutions and zigzags. Wanklyn sensed, then saw, an aircraft over-head. The escort returned at full speed, dropping depth-charges. She neared the scene.

"Dive deep," Wanklyn ordered, still barely a trace of excitement or emotion in his voice. Once more they were deaf and blind.

Twenty-six depth-charges—ashcans, they were called

—cracked and crashed around them, some dull and muffled. All the while Wanklyn could not know by listening gear or periscope what the escort would do next. The enemy escort kept up the attack all afternoon. The sunk ship turned out to be a Vichy tanker, so Wanklyn had decided right.

Upholder now had only about forty-eight hours to go before she could expect her recall to Malta. Unless the recall signal did not reach her, as in the case of old Collett! She had carried out two satisfactory attacks, which left her with two torpedoes. One of these was the leaky specimen discovered on the first day out from base. But by now, despite the depth-charges and other diversions occupying the torpedo crew, they had made it tight. The other torpedo was in the tube that could not be fired in the first attack—so the ordeal of unloading and reloading was tackled again. And all the time the sub. had to contend with the swell which constant watch at periscope depth involved.

After the reloading every one aboard was genuinely pleased that the swell on the sea increased so much as to put periscope watch out of the question. So *Upholder* was able to drop into the depths comfortably and with a clear conscience. The respite proved a relief to the crew and, as things turned out, helped them for what was to come. Meanwhile the sub. stayed deep, waiting for the weather to moderate.

Mid-afternoon. Nerves were suddenly strung to action pitch by totally unexpected explosions of depth-charges in the vicinity. It needed no mechanical aids to detect those reverberating concussions.

"Better have a look," Wanklyn ordered. But a return to periscope depth revealed nothing.

"Couldn't see much, anyway, in this weather," he muttered, gazing at the stormy scene in the lens, and giving a Scottish shrug. So *Upholder* retired to the peace of deeper waters for the second time while the mysterious bombardment went on. The P.O. tele-graphist recorded twenty-one charges that afternoon, till at tea-time they stopped as suddenly as they had begun.

"Four o'clock, eh? P'raps they've gone 'ome for a cupper!" said a London wag in the mess-deck.

Wanklyn went back to his cabin for a short spell. He tried to sleep, but could not. He took up a book for relaxation. But after a while he gave it up and returned to Crawford.

"Swell seems a bit better, sir."

"Yes. We'll pop up and take a peep."

Nothing was in sight. Knowing that they would be leaving the area that night, Wanklyn moved slowly southward along the enemy's route on the off-chance of coming across a target for the last two torpedoes. The hope seemed slight. The two previous attacks—more or less in midstream—must surely have scared whatever traffic there might be about close to the coast. But nothing was even coast-hugging. A submariner's life was one long game of chance, though—the secret of its appeal to men like Wanklyn. He had only to see the slightest sign of an opening and he would streak in to the attack.

The gathering gloom of twilight appeared to the east, beyond the heaving, cruel sea. The patrol looked like drawing to its close quietly. This was one of the two periods during the day when it is too light for a sub. to stay on the surface safely, yet too dark to see through the periscope properly. The evening and dawn periods could be most awkward of all for the commanding officer. So the plan adopted was for the sub. to stay deep until surface conditions seemed safe for a proper look-out to be kept. Before sunrise and after sunset a good look-round was made, and then the sub. dived deep till it was light enough to see through the periscope or sufficiently dark to surface without fear of the small silhouette being sighted.

The sun set on May 24, 1941. Wanklyn's watch showed 2020. He swung the periscope round slowly, as if reluctant to go deep and await the comforting darkness.

This was the moment when the V.C. action really began.

For a few hours later—though he did not know it—Wanklyn would have done enough to justify receiving the Victoria Cross.

How did this start? He sighted a speck in the sky: nothing else. An aircraft patrolling to the northward. He held on for a few minutes longer. Still the swell took *Upholder* with it, to and fro. Depth-keeping was difficult. *Upholder* 'pumped' up and down. The horizon seemed shadowy, indistinct, to the east; blood-red, clear-cut to the west. The storm clouds banked up westward. One moment the horizon would be startlingly close; then the sub. fell away in a trough, and the swell raced by the top window of the periscope, blotting out everything except the darkening waters.

Ten minutes passed. Then, at 2030, strongly silhouetted against the afterglow of sunset, Wanklyn suddenly saw three large two-funnel transports tearing at top speed on a south-westerly course.

"Ships, Tubby—three of them."

Wanklyn thought in a flash: *light failing, so periscope practically useless; listening gear out of order; only two torpedoes left*. Yet none of these factors deterred him. He may also have glimpsed the top-masts of destroyers, but the swell made seeing more and more difficult each minute. Yet the more impossible the conditions the better Wanklyn was; he would rise to the challenge— whereas once he unaccountably missed an unescorted target from close range.

This time he did not stop to see if the enemy were escorted or not. He was too intent to close, close, as fast as he could. But he knew that ships such as these would not be sailing alone. Light bad, sea bad, time short— and getting worse and shorter. No time to start a plot to get the enemy's speed.

"They're liners, I should think—getting on for twenty thousand. One's a bit bigger than the rest," Wanklyn announced, as he studied them for a second in the dusk. The troop transports—which was what they were— sailed in a line at a speed of some twenty knots, aiming for Africa. He followed them for four minutes, then they altered course conveniently more towards *Upholder*. Seeing that all would be well—or, at least, that they were coming in his direction—Wanklyn took time for a fleeting spin round with the periscope. The only thing to be said for the weather was that it made the enemy unlikely to spot a periscope among the heaving sea.

Then Wanklyn spoke:

"Here they are, Tubby. Destroyers. Four or five of them. Didn't see them before. They're screening the convoy. Curse those empty tubes. Two torpedoes left and a target like this. Have to shorten the range. Don't know their speed sufficiently to go ahead yet."

He shortened the attack still further, brought the sub. round towards the oncoming ships looming in the last light of day, screwed up his eyes to make sure where they were—and read off bearings on all of them.

He estimated speeds again, checked directions, compared them to *Upholder's*; then he changed course.

This marked the start of the assault. He had to hit first time with one of the two torpedoes. An audacious attack by one deaf and blind sub. on seven or eight big ships—four or five armed to their topmast and full of fatal ashcans. *Upholder* practically skated through the destroyer screen.

2032. It was dusk now, and eyes were all but blind. Wanklyn manœuvred *Upholder* into the precise position planned for an attack at short range. No good the long-off attack. And surfacing would be suicide. So Wanklyn got *Upholder* right in among the enemy. He peered through the periscope, swivelled it slightly, and saw the first of the transports. Then the second. He had no idea where the enemy escorts were. Only that five destroyers roamed at large. The danger of being rammed remained in his mind. The water washed against the top window of the periscope.

2033. Wanklyn gave the order: "Fire." The torpedoes slid out of the tubes; their backlash shivered through the sub. Then, as the two torpedoes left, Wanklyn saw a huge black V heading straight for the sub.—the bows of a destroyer thirty seconds' steaming off, and getting nearer each second.

"Crash dive," he shouted, and added: "Deep."

Down, down, down, went *Upholder*, while Wanklyn

counted off the seconds from the time the torpedoes left. Fifteen, thirty, forty-five seconds. One minute. Seventy-seven seconds—then two mild explosions. But the same short interval separated them as the firing of the torpedoes from the tubes. They heard the bangs without the aid of their 'ears.'

Then, about a hundred and fifty seconds after, came the first of the battering bursts of the depth-charges. The lights flickered; shades splintered across the deck; men were caught off balance, and groped for support. *Upholder* twisted and turned. The second, third, and fourth charges spluttered through the deep. Wanklyn could only guess where the destroyers were, or which way they headed. It was a lethal game of blind-man's-bluff on either side—except that the ships must know roughly where *Upholder* was wriggling.

Down the depth-charges came. Nearly two a minute shattered the water around *Upholder's* hull for minutes on end; and all the while Wanklyn cocked his ears to the direction of the charges, gauged the positions of the attackers, and steered his sub. as far from them as he could. Even so, some depth-charges exploded close enough to break the bulbs and knock other odd bits of equipment across the deck. The whole area sounded as if it were being subjected to systematic depth-charging. But by a miracle, almost, Wanklyn dodged them all— through split-second navigation and course-changing. The sub. traced a crazy zigzag at different depths—like a wild animal threatened with a trap, determined to be free.

Thirty-three charges came in nineteen minutes. Then they heard—without their aids—the ominous, thunderous beat of propellers as the hunter hurried overhead. Nerve-shattering seconds that got worse and worse as the throbbing and threshing of the props grew louder, louder, louder, till they were racing directly above the sub.

Every man in *Upholder* was sweating now. But the sound passed its climax. Then they heard the plop of the charges as they hit the water. How near *Upholder*? Thirty-three lives depended on the answer, as they waited and waited. For if you hear props by ear it is too late to try to escape—you're right below them.

Four final shattering cracks. *Upholder* lurched. Men felt funny in their throats—and stomachs. "Thirty-seven charges in nineteen minutes" was what the log-entry read. Just that. The last quartet came nearest of all. Anyone not steeled to the ordeal would have had broken blood-vessels.

But it passed. Then silence. Strange, intense silence, as after a storm.

Half an hour later nerves were challenged again. Even Crawford felt in a tensed-up frame of mind. He told Tanner so afterwards. A series of light tapping noises sounded like a sweep wire passing over the hull. The mystery was not solved. They assumed that the noise must have come somehow from the sinking ship and was not a sweep.

The next decision for Wanklyn to take was to choose between escape—and the danger of using his motors at any speed. The sound of engines gave their position away when the attackers came too close. So he stopped engines completely for an hour. Not a sound broke the stillness. Thirty-three men sat silent near the bed of the Mediterranean: Wanklyn, three months a lieutenant-commander, looking tired but happy, having outwitted five destroyers; Tubby Crawford checking a navigation point; the two sub-lieutenants, too young to be mixed up in all this, Wanklyn thought; and twenty-eight others.

"Serve some tea," Wanklyn whispered. And Chef pressed his messmates to mugs of hot tea and slices of cake—and the last of the fresh fruit salad.

"Needn't have bothered about the hot water—we're in it already," a wag said.

Chef made them eat. "Remember what they say," he urged, "a balanced and complete diet—essential for us submariners."

By the time the meal was over the enemy had evidently given up the hunt—at least, for the night. It was 2200. Nothing could be heard. If ever anyone felt cut off from the rest of the world *Upholder*'s company did this day. They were in a static submarine with no listening gear, and it was night-time above. The world might just as well not have existed.

Wanklyn thought of Betty back in Scotland. It seemed like another life.

"Periscope depth," he decided. He grabbed the handles eagerly, and scanned the horizon round its three hundred and sixty degrees—but the periscope was practically useless at night.

"Stand by to surface," was the sign for a muted cheer from the crew. They came up where the transport had gone down. There was nothing to be heard in the gloom as Wanklyn clambered on to the bridge, but the breeze blowing across the heaving waters wafted a strong smell of fuel-oil. The moon came from behind a cloud and lit fragments of wood, broken boats, and flotsam—all that remained above water of the 17,800-ton transport *Conte Rosso*.

F

"Strange to think, Tubby," Wanklyn mused, as they charged batteries and breathed in the oily night air, "she's lying on the bottom just below us somewhere. She might easily have touched us. Perhaps that was what the noise was. We might have been there too, with a bit of bad luck."

"Thanks for getting us out of it," Crawford said simply.

They set sail for Malta. They were already sure of having sunk the ship, but the certainty was confirmed a few days later by a lifeboat, bearing the name *Conte Rosso*, of a large ship being washed up on a remote part of the island.

The official communiqué described the action in superlative terms. "With the greatest courage, coolness and skill he brought *Upholder* clear of the enemy and back to harbour."

The Wanklyn legend continued to be 'writ in water,' and the tonnage sunk by *Upholder* steadily grew. Then, several months later, Wanklyn received his recognition of the *Conte Rosso* episode.

Geoffrey Tanner, the staff officer, had the pleasant privilege of breaking the news. He knocked on Wanklyn's cabin door ashore without response. Tanner tiptoed inside and tried to rouse the master submariner and get him to take an intelligent interest in things at half-past four in the morning.

"Starfy" stumbled across the darkened cabin.

"Wanklyn! I say, Wanklyn, old man," he whispered.

But the man whose youthful years had carried and was still carrying such a strain was now ashore and asleep. Tanner realized that his senses must be specially dulled for his liberty time at base. At sea he would have awoken at the slightest sign of anything in the nature of a call or shake. Now it was different.

"Wanklyn! You old so-an'-so!" bellowed Tanner.

Finally the figure stirred and rolled over on to his back.

"What is it?"

"It's just that I wanted to be the first to congratulate you. You've got the V.C.!"

"Good lord." Wanklyn was wide awake. "Impossible. They can't have."

"The cypher office phoned through to me just now. I came right along."

Wanklyn lay motionless for a moment, and then said in a quiet voice:

"I *am* glad, Starfy. It's a wonderful surprise. And thanks for coming along."

Geoffrey Tanner grinned and leaned over to put a hand on Wanklyn's shoulder. Then he left the cabin.

When Wanklyn awoke he sent a telegram to Perthshire: "Betty darling. I have got two tails and they are both wagging hard. All my love. David Wanklyn."

The award was first announced on the 6 P.M. news bulletin of the B.B.C. that same day. Betty sat by her radio waiting to hear it—for the second post had brought her an expressed letter addressed from the Submarine H.Q. at Northways, London:

DEAR MRS WANKLYN,

I have been officially told that the Admiralty are sending a telegram to-day to your husband saying that H.M. the King has conferred the Victoria Cross on him in recognition of his most gallant actions and successes in *Upholder*. I want to be among the first to congratulate you. Everybody in submarines will be equally delighted

as I am for we know better than others the measure of his
sustained courage and skill. With all good wishes.

Yours sincerely,

MAX HORTON

PS.—When I saw your husband some six weeks ago he
was looking very well and both he and his officers and
men were in splendid spirit.

The award underlined the words of the Prime
Minister in the House of Commons that same week:

"Half and sometimes more, of everything—men,
munitions and fuel—which the enemy sends to Africa,
is sunk before it gets there."

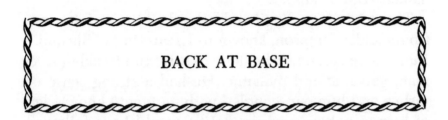

9

BACK AT BASE

Wanklyn certainly created chances; but, even with his genius, patrols relapsed into routine for much of the time. Yet regular routine work at sea depended on still more routine back at base. Not a sub. could put to sea without the work of the men on Malta. And gradually, as will soon be seen, conditions on the island became more and more intolerable. Now it was summer, though, and the base staff continued in comparative peace: deploying the submarines strategically; maintaining them efficient and ready for sea at a second's notice; looking after the comfort of the crews when they came in from patrol wan and worn; and generally keeping things going behind the scenes.

A submarine depot 'ship'—ashore or afloat—is normally planned as a hotel, workshop, and general store, to house, repair, and supply a specific number of subs. A department exists for every need, with a head for each.

In 1941 this happy ideal was far from applying at the sub. base of Lazaretto. In fact, the nucleus of it had to grow up actually as the subs. carried on with their side of the business. It grew, was altered, and adapted; was hit and repaired—all amid good humour and the usual amount of red tape, even in Malta under siege. Yet one fine day that summer the rambling conglomeration of buildings became a ship, which was commissioned and named H.M.S. *Talbot*.

The driving, guiding hand behind all the activity was Commander Simpson, known to Lazaretto as "Shrimp." Full justice can never be done to this little freckle-faced man, galvanic and dynamic. He had a strong sense of justice and humour, coupled with an innate knowledge of human nature; and the flotilla would have followed him cheerfully to kingdom come, had he ordained it. Simpson was utterly to be depended on, and he trusted men to behave as he would have them do—and they usually did.

Censure came rarely, even when it was earned or expected. A commanding officer might return from patrol kicking himself for an opportunity lost and fearing the worst from his commander. But Shrimp Simpson merely pointed out any errors and omissions. He always made allowance for the youth and inexperience of his crews, for the excitement of the moment when split-second decisions had to be taken under such stress.

"Never mind, old man," Simpson said more than once. "Lots more targets left—you'll clock one next time."

This was far more effective than a reprimand. And away would go the commanding officer concerned, relieved and his self-confidence restored. As Geoffrey Tanner put it to Shrimp on one occasion: "You've smoothed his fur the right way again, sir; better than getting him all ruffled."

As well as his other qualities, Simpson really got

things done. He learnt how to improvise at Harwich during the invasion scares of 1940, so he was the ideal man to take charge of sub. matters at Malta—where improvisation was the order of the day every day. Simpson had tremendous responsibilities, too, for he was cut off from contact with his Commander-in-Chief and also Admiral (Submarines) except through radio channels and the mail. The radio was congested at all times; the mail often did not exist for weeks on end. So it was just as well that Simpson's habit proved not to ask advice but to act, and then if necessary report or account for what had been done. His monthly letters, although official, recorded everything that happened not in cold terms but with a warm human approach.

Only Simpson knew how heavily his responsibilities weighed on him; he never showed a sign in public. More than once he joined in the noisy, gusty life of a mess evening with his usual infectious spirits, while only he and Tanner knew that one of the flotilla was long over-due and both of them feared her loss. A couple of times, perhaps, during the evening Tanner's eyes would meet Simpson's, and for a second they were silent; but the bond must not be broken. They both understood. For these other men in the mess would soon be going back to the underwater world where anything might happen. Simpson's was no pose or an effort to forget, but he knew that his bearing was the barometer for the whole flotilla. If it showed 'set fair,' then that was what things were. And the life of *Talbot* went on with its usual zest and jest.

This spirit Simpson subtly infused into the flotilla extended also to other individuals living in Malta who had little connexion with the submarines. An inspiring indirect compliment to Simpson was written by a non-submariner officer of Malta base staff at the end of the term of his first association with the Lazaretto subs., the people who manned them, and the work they did:

> I would like to express my pride at having been associated with submarines, the Tenth Submarine Flotilla in particular. It has given me an insight into modern warfare at sea, applied with a rare mixture of venom, ability and gay abandon by young officers under the guidance of experienced and understanding staff officers.
>
> The experience gained in watching plans unfold, aided by initiative and determination allied to a glorious sense of humour, has left its mark on me.
>
> Above all, those two years spent with submarines will always keep me young in spirit and general outlook.

The writer showed remarkable insight into the tone of the flotilla when he contributed that 'unsolicited testimonial.'

On a wet and windy evening early in that first winter, while the raids were gathering momentum, Lieutenant-Commander (E.) S. A. MacGregor brought a breath of Caledonia to the beleaguered isle. He had journeyed to Malta by submarine—appropriately—and cruiser on his second 'make-do and mend' job in twelve months, for like Simpson he too had served at Harwich in the dark days.

MacGregor sat in an uncomfortable armchair drawn close to a temperamental wood fire spurting smoke into a cheerless, draughty, stone-flagged ante-room. He was not amused. But gradually MacGregor got the fire going better, and by the end of the evening could warm his hands by it without having his face covered in smoke. All done by Scottish perseverance.

MacGregor knew what submarines wanted and, come hell or Hitler, he was going to see that they got it. An epic episode, a sort of one-man-band who kept on and on through good days and bad.

Like Simpson, MacGregor proved a great cutter of red tape. "Do first and ask after" was the watchword at Lazaretto. The War came first. Where it was difficult they just had to get round the regulations. This outlook gave good results generally, but inevitably caused heart-burning and resentment in the dockyard departments bound by red tape hand and foot. True, they turned a Nelsonian eye to Admiralty officialdom on occasion; but twenty-five years of peace-time living according to the regulations were too much to overlook always. For the officious officials still sometimes found in the dockyard the War took second place to their rules.

The real sticklers were some of the local departmental clerks, who, like characters in Kipling, insisted on every-thing being just so! But "Sam" MacGregor soon found that a signature worked wonders. All regulations worried him when he was wanting to get something done quickly—and forms were absolute anathema! To his huge satisfaction, a bomb of the largest calibre found its final resting place in the dockyard stationery store! Demand forms, supply forms, receipt forms, requisition forms, forms, forms, and still more forms lay either scorched or scattered. Miles away, at Birchikara, local residents picked them up and turned them over to the police, thinking that a leaflet-raid had been in progress! Sam was satisfied. One of his ambitions had been realized. But the battle was still far from won.

The little details took the time, MacGregor found. Take the cases of the half-round bastards and the nails. He needed a particular type of file. It was semicircular in cross-section, and by its official name would appear to have originated out of wedlock! Summoning all his strength, he sat down in his little office, read all the instructions, and with a supreme effort managed to make out the requisite number of demand notes, correct down to the last detail.

With all duly signed and counter-signed, they were sent off to the dockyard. Sam sighed with relief and turned to other work with a sense of duty well done. He had only to await the arrival of a number of half-round bastards. To his dismay, the messenger returned complete with the forms to report that there were none available.

Sam shrugged his shoulders and let it go at that. He had a week to get some, but a sub. could not sail until he did. Next day Sam was in the dockyard on other business, but, being near the storehouse where he knew files were kept, he paused and went inside. The storekeeper might have made a mistake, he thought, or misread his admittedly bad hand-writing on the demand notes. But there was no mistake.

"Ow, Sinjeu! Spitcher files! Mundux!" wailed the storekeeper, waving his hands about as he beckoned MacGregor to an empty bin labelled in white letters— Files, bastard, half-round.

Sam admitted defeat in the face of such evidence, but nosed around behind the scenes while the storekeeper fulfilled some other order.

Suddenly Sam let out a yell of rage as his eyes fell on a bin bursting with beautiful, brand-new files—bastard, half-round. His bellow brought the agitated storekeeper scampering back to him.

"What the hell are these, then? Thought you said you hadn't any bastards!"

"Ow, Sinjeu," retorted the keeper. "Not for issue! Emergency stock—have ordered more, but not come yet, Sinjeu!"

"Well, I'll be——"

After some softer explanation and a few signatures MacGregor returned to Lazaretto with the files. And work went on.

So much for the files. Now for the nails! This time Sam delved into the difficult realms of local purchase. He needed some nails large and long enough for driving into the rock walls. They were not available from official sources, so he was authorized by the regulations to buy what he wanted locally.

An ironmonger in Valletta had just the thing, so Sam bought some and asked 'Admiralty Authority' for his money back. But Authority was not to be put off as easily as that. A miniature mound of correspondence piled up, pointing out that you could not do things this way at all. It was all most irregular. Several firms should be approached first to make tenders, and then Authority would arrange for samples to be surveyed to see that the goods came up to the specified standard.

However, Authority was prepared to take a lenient view on this one occasion, as the nails were now actually in use and appeared to be carrying out their function satisfactorily. But a properly receipted bill must be forthcoming before any consideration could be given to refunding the purchase price—or even a part thereof!

By the time that the correspondence had reached this

stage the nails were nearly rusted through and some required replacement. But Sam was a Scot, dogged and dour. And it was getting to be a matter primarily of principle. So he went back to the ironmonger to ask for a receipt for the nails he had bought many Mediterranean moons ago. The storekeeper was slightly bewildered, but produced a receipt which was duly forwarded to Authority. Sam chuckled as he read it:

"To: lot of nails—1s. 3d."

A Scottish victory on points.

Early on, there were no Heads of Departments, because there were no Departments. MacGregor served as Jack-of-all-trades, and master of all, too. A first lieutenant wanted paint; a P.O. telegraphist's radio went wrong; both went to Sam. Battery troubles, gun troubles, stores—all got adequate attention. He kept the subs. ready for sea and improved the base amenities at the same time. Somehow. A small team of Maltese workmen under the active co-operation of their foreman, Mr Brincat, helped him. Old buildings, new needs. MacGregor supervised it all and took the well-meaning suggestions of the base staff with a pinch of salt.

"I know ye want a comfortable suite—but there are such things as subs. to consider, as well as the comfort of shore staff, d'ye ken?"

A great source of supply was found in the form of the badly damaged canteen at the destroyer depot on the other side of the island.

"There are no destroyers to use it," Mac said to Simpson before the quartet arrived, "and it would be a crime to leave its contents to rot until finally wiped out by the Luftwaffe. And the stuff could be put to such guid use over here!"

"All right, Sam—you've convinced me," Simpson agreed—Simpson, now with a fourth ring on each arm signifying his recent promotion to Captain. Prompt recognition of the work being done by *Talbot* personnel at Malta and in the Mediterranean.

The finest acquisition by far was a cinema projector and several hundred seats.

"A ready-made Ritz if ever I saw one," MacGregor enthused. "It'll be worth its weight, mark my words." In no time at all a store-room had been cleared, the screen erected, projector mounted, seats installed, and the 'Lazaritz' was doing capacity business for two shows a day at 4.30 and 8.30, with two changes of programme per week. The Malta cinema managers lent willingly from their large libraries of films, and the cinema became one of the boons in the harder times. It sustained spirits for sixpence a time.

The apple of MacGregor's eye was his bagpipes. Next in order came the workshop. At first, with literally no facilities for repairs at Lazaretto, a lot of time was being lost in getting done in the dockyard all the many minor maintenance jobs needed for subs. returning from patrol.

It was the Scot's aim to make Lazaretto self-supporting. A couple of benches with vices would have been something, but there was nothing—till MacGregor got going with his idea of a workshop. He managed to clear a store-room, lay a concrete floor, and install lighting and a power-shaft. Then the question of equipment arose.

No spare machine-tools existed in Malta, naturally—nor could they be supplied by the dockyard, then busy moving itself underground to avoid the raids. But MacGregor went on asking for a lathe or two, a drilling machine, a small forge, keeping his requests reasonable. He never had any luck at all until a sharp raid on the dockyard put several machine-shops out of action. On his next visit to the area affected his usual request was met with an airy gesture of the hand, like the wave of a wand to him, and the magic words:

"Take whatever you can find, old fellow!"

Surveying the heaps of rubble, Sam's eyes glowed as he visualized what lay beneath. He was sure that something could be salvaged. He hurried back to Lazaretto, collected the local lorry, and all the 'hands' he could waylay or press-gang—and set to work. Whipped up by his enthusiasm, they worked wonderfully among the remains, and that very day the foundation was laid for the Palace of Engineering which had already taken shape in MacGregor's mind.

From this fortunate start in the spring an efficient little workshop steadily got into its stride, bearing the nameplate of "Lazaretto Industries Inc." in bold letters across the door. A team of Maltese artisans moved in and quickly settled down.

One of the first actions of these Maltese was to install in the workshop a little shrine, which was illuminated day and night, first by a tiny paraffin lamp and later by electricity. Of all the straggling buildings in Lazaretto connected with the submarine base that workshop was in due course the only one which suffered not a single speck of damage from enemy action. . . .

The Maltese took immense pride in their association with H.M.S. *Talbot*, and their sun-swarthy faces flashed with wild excitement whenever a sub. returned flying a 'Jolly Roger' signifying success.

As all the submarines were identical U-class vessels,

some scenes inevitably occurred of mistaken identity.
One day an infuriated Chief Engine Room Artificer of
P32 came rushing up to MacGregor.

"Why on earth have that crowd of meddling Maltese
started to pull my beautiful engines to pieces behind
my back, sir?"

"Wait a minute, Chief," MacGregor said swiftly.
Then it dawned on him.

"I'm sorry, but I told them to go and cure some asth-
matic trouble or other that there's been on P34. They
must have got their numbers mixed!"

"Well, all right, sir," said the chief, realizing that he
had been a bit hasty with a two-and-a-half-ringer!

This similarity between all the U-subs. and also all the
P-subs. was the cause of averting a crisis, though, before
the supply of spare parts became adequate. Often they
had to rip out an essential piece of one sub. and put it
into another before she could go on patrol.

As in the case of the deck-tube insulator. To get the
main wireless aerial down into a submarine, it is passed
through a tube in the pressure-hull surmounted by a
large porcelain insulator, an unhandy and unhappy
affair which was liable occasionally to crack, especially
during depth-charging. Cracking, of course, let in water
where it was not wanted, and at the least sign of damage
these insulators had to be replaced.

Upholder returned from patrol with a piece chipped
out of her insulator, after a fierce counter-attack, and no
spare was available. MacGregor then had one of his
frequent inspirations—born out of necessity—and un-
shipped the insulator, had it humped along to the dental
surgery, and persuaded an astounded "Toothie" to try
his skill on it! Despite all the drills at the surgeon's

disposal, the insensibility of the patient made a permanent repair impossible. By this time *Upholder* was due to put to sea again.

"What'll we do, Sam?" Wanklyn asked the ever-ingenious engineer, who was far from defeated yet.

"I know, David—we'll borrow the insulator from P33 and pop your defective one in her for a while."

And so it went on. Each time that the defective insulator became due for a spell at sea it was replaced by the one from the sub. last in from patrol. Until one day the organization got caught on the wrong foot—and all available submarines were ordered to sea together. So there was nothing for it. The damaged insulator went with the unfortunate sub. it happened to be in at the time. Despite this, though, it gave good service for many more patrols.

Petty problems such as these were meat and drink to MacGregor, and when his workshop reached full operational order his ingenuity was directed into still more diverse channels, not always official!

After a raid near Lazaretto Geoffrey Tanner hurried over to survey any damage. And he paused for a poignant moment as he rounded a corner near MacGregor's cabin. Fortunately, Mac had not been in it at the time of the raid, but Tanner now saw his hairy torso and brick-red countenance emerging triumphantly from the bombed remains of the cabin—a pile of blasted rock—waving the salvaged remnants of his beloved bagpipes.

Tanner remembered that moment beyond many Malta memories. True, all the instrument's components were retrieved, but the bag itself proved practically unrepairable. MacGregor surveyed the clean-cut rent

PERISCOPE PATROL

IMAGES

The Jolly Roger flying from a submarine masthead, with chevrons to show the number of ships she has sunk.
(Crown copyright)

Flotilla Commander Captain G. W. G. "Shrimp" Simpson, C.B., C.B.E, commanded all operations of the 10th Submarine Flotilla with brilliant success.
(Crown copyright)

Wanklyn, V.C., with beard flanked by his three officers of *Upholder*.
This most famous of all submarines lies alongside as a fitting background.
(Imperial War Museum)

Looking out through an age-old arch of the Lazaretto, the base of Malta submarines throughout their sixteen months' saga.
(Crown copyright)

Officers snatching a few hours' rest ashore from the perpetual patrols – but still within sight of their submarines.
(Crown copyright)

M. Submarine *Unrivalled*, sleek in the sun, returning to Malta after patrol. Later on all submarines
d to stay submerged against air attack. *(Crown copyright)*

Class submarine alongside in Lazaretto creek. *(Crown copyright)*

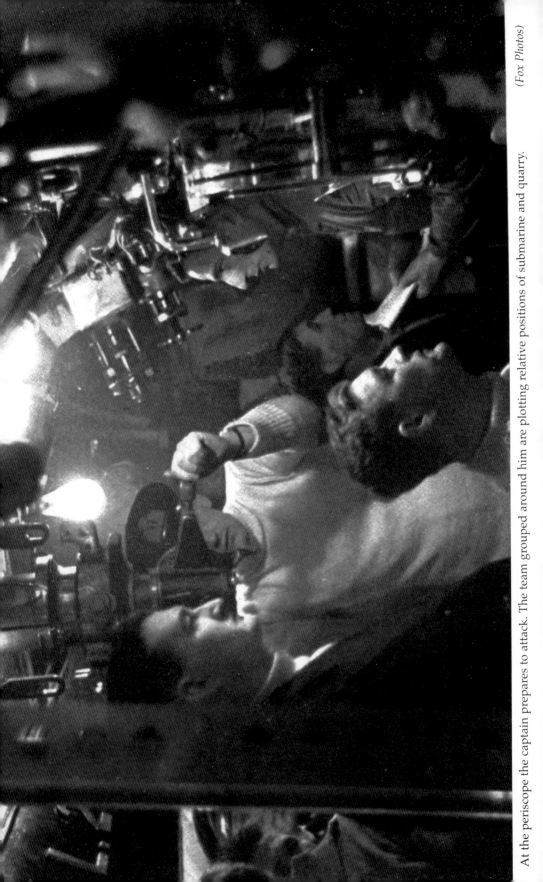

At the periscope the captain prepares to attack. The team grouped around him are plotting relative positions of submarine and quarry. *(Fox Photos)*

Confined quarters on the mess deck. The crew play cribbage to while away a quiet hour. Space is so short that the loaves of bread have to be stored overhead among the hammocks.
(Imperial War Museum)

Loading a torpedo into its tube with not an inch of space to spare. Just one of a hundred hazards in the life of a submarine at war.
(Imperial War Museum)

Air assault on Malta: The base being hit by one of many Luftwaffe raids. Submarine crews had to contend with this ashore after long, dangerous patrols in the Mediterranean.

Enemy ship going down off the coast of Sicily, photographed through the periscope of one of the submarines operating from Malta. *(Imperial War Museum*

from all aspects and then set to work with patches and compounds of his own Highland brewing! But to no avail. None were enough to maintain the pressure. As a last resort, he took the precious thing along to the sick bay and besought the surgeon to have a go with needle and thread. But this failed on actual trial. And an ersatz bag, from a Maltese goat, produced noises which would have insulted the ear of even a stone-deaf or tone-deaf Scot—let alone a MacGregor!

Salvation came in the shape of a ship, the valiant *Breconshire*, who ran many cargoes into hard-pressed Malta. An ironic name to bring succour to a Scotsman! MacGregor went aboard, and with a little explanation, cajolery, and perhaps a whiff of whisky, he finally enlisted the sympathy of a brother Scot, who was persuaded to part with one of his two spares for bagpipes. MacGregor bore it back to Lazaretto in triumph, where the skirl of the pipes once more mellowed the savage Scottish breast!

All successful ship's engineers in fiction are Scotsmen. MacGregor, O.B.E., R.N., proved that they are just as sound in fact.

Another base officer indispensable to Lazaretto was Lieutenant-Commander R. Giddings. After years of retirement spent in Malta connected with a well-known wine and spirit company he was recalled for service in 1939 and eventually gravitated to Lazaretto to become First Lieutenant of the sub. base. His knowledge of local conditions and characteristics, coupled with his business connexions, proved the vital liaison between the British and Maltese. Strolling round the base at all hours, its piggery, rabbitry, and gardens, he could get Maltese

G

ratings to work harder and faster than anyone else could, and long after his shadow had passed their particular scene. They knew he was of Malta.

Miners excavating shelters once found their progress held up by an accumulation of débris. Giddings soon got things organized. A stream of Maltese sailors, stewards, and cooks trickled in and out of the place like an ant colony, with little barrows full of rubble or else carrying great chunks of rock on their shoulders. "Into the diggings," Mr Giddings had said. So into them they went.

How he managed to conjure the champagne to celebrate births and decorations was one of the unrevealed secrets of the siege of Malta. At about half-past two on the afternoon of a Lazaretto party Giddings would vanish with his faithful wine-steward, Agius. During the next four hours innumerable ingredients of varying potency were mixed in a vast metal tub—and by half-past six the party would open with plentiful supplies of 'Giddings' Special.'

The Lazaretto parties became an institution in the halcyon days of 1941. Every one eagerly looked forward to them. They were given every six weeks or so with the specific purpose of repaying in some measure the hospitality shown by so many people whose homes were on the island.

It was essential for as many submariners as possible to get right away from the sight and sound of war when they came ashore off patrol—particularly commanding officers. And, small as Malta is, it was amazing how far away one could get, and how many people—from the Governor down—who kept open house for any submariner wanting a rest. The hosts and hostesses of

Malta, local or British, played a great part in providing rest, recuperation, and recreation.

A great number of guests always appeared at the parties, even though the glamour of a ship rigged for a peace-time At Home was missing. For, despite all difficulties, the indefatigable Torpedo Party produced coloured lights and bunting, soft music, and a hundred and one exciting corners diplomatically left unlit in the labyrinth which was Lazaretto!

Guests gathered in the long arched veranda running the entire length of the officers' block, and watched later arrivals disembarking directly under the veranda. It was a romantic scene on a brave, beleaguered isle.

At summer sundown many might linger after 'blackout' signalled a general move to the mess. Those who stayed outside saw the outer bastions of Valletta vividly reflecting the sunset in splendour for a few magic moments. Red tints mirrored in the glassy waters of the harbour . . . then the bastion in grimmest grey . . . and lastly as a black mass in an indigo sky.

And indoors the party was working up to a climax. Wanklyn, the man with piercing, penetrating eyes, calm concentration, and quiet charm, was enjoying himself as much as any one—if slightly more restrained. The mess was waxing hilarious. Some of the submariners grabbed the set of snooker balls and celebrated Wanklyn's V.C. by filling his trousers with them. Three of the reds rolled right down and potted themselves out of sight under a chair!

The room rang with young joyous shouts as a figure swathed in a sarong and crowned with a tarboosh swept through the door. Then a hush as the self-styled Sheikh of Hammaneggs plumped into a chair, struck a chord on an anachronistic mouth-organ, and slapped his knees with his hands, shouting:

"Bring on the dancing girls—I would be amused!"

Captain Simpson kept the fun going loud and long. Then Cayley, the lanky Wanklyn, and spade-bearded Collett offered their rendering of "Three Turtle Doves." And the trio's voices drifted down far beyond the shuttered windows to the water, barely stirring in the stillness of the night.

Even the dour Agius behind the bar-hatch could not suppress a smile at the two and a bit yards of Tommo shimmering in to give his turn as a one-armed flautist.

"Jairmany Calling" was the signal that young Poole was warming up with one of his realistic bulletins concocted on the spur of the moment—with local allusions to Malta being sunk without trace!

More turns: Collett, Wanklyn, and Pat Norman clambered on to three chairs to give their inimitable impression of a Dornier bombing London, while a slight rearrangement resulted in a mock attack on a U-boat.

This was Lazaretto in those halcyon days and nights of 1941. A spontaneous spark of survival. A gesture to the Germans that the island was immortal.

10

AFTER the Lazaretto party they went back to patrol. Often the officers would be in the mess at midnight and doing their trim dive at dawn. The parties proved vital for that very reason: the crews could not have gone on and on without their periods ashore, although in the next winter of '41–'42 things got so hot on Malta that the subs. were as safe as a billet ashore—even when they were out on patrol.

During these perpetual patrols the submarine slid slowly along at periscope depth. In the crowded control-room the captain, standing at the periscope, watched the empty Mediterranean. The first lieutenant, jacket over a polo-necked sweater, had his eyes on the depth-gauges. A foot in front of him stood the two planesmen, operating the hydroplanes that control the depth. The captain was coatless—but had his cap on; and the strong electric light threw the faces and figures of the quartet into dramatic outline.

Away in the engine-room men were checking the machinery, bank on bank of it, crammed into this area— pistons, gauges, valves, pipes. And for'ard in the mess some of the men off duty grouped around a long, narrow table, in overalls, jerseys, or anything else. Four or five each side of the table, with hammocks swinging head-high above them. Day and night quarters, living and sleeping, in that small dim world below the sea.

The conditions on this particular day seemed perfect for an attack. A fresh wind whipped the white horses in the bright sunlight. The reflected blue of the sea and sky glowed in the eyepieces as the captain craned to see around the unrelieved horizon. But the wind was not enough to hide the periscope's plume of water, the only real break in the surface of the sea. The only thing missing now was a target. The captain paused to tear off a shred of tissue-paper and wipe the moisture from the lenses. Then again, with head and shoulders bent forward, he peered into the periscope.

"Ah, here we are."

In the control-room the diving watch on duty heard his quiet, casual words.

"Yes, this is it—two of 'em—oh, lovely. Down periscope."

The instrument hissed downward until its lower end disappeared into the well that housed it. All hands closed up to action stations; the torpedo-tubes were brought to the ready; the attack team huddled around the captain. Silence again.

"Up periscope."

The captain crouched almost on his knees to seize the handles and get his eyes to the instrument. It rose till the upper window reappeared in the sunshine. He looked at the target for the second time, and in the same unhurried tone began to call out the attack data—bearing, angle on the bow, range. The attack was on. To the original four around the periscope was added another. The P.O. telegraphist—pencil and pad in hand —stared straight at the captain as he went into the assault, and logged every event from the first sighting on.

A week later, after the submarine's return, Captain Simpson received the bald narrative of this attack:

1240. Sighted two supply ships approaching on a course for Bizerta. Two ships later seen to be one supply-ship of about 4000 tons, and one medium-size tanker, disposed in line abreast, with two torpedo-boats on either bow as escort. Unfortunately the tanker was on the far side from the sub., and the other vessel had to be the target.

1330. In position 38°20′ N., 12°35′ E. Fired four torpedoes.

1332½. Two explosions at an interval corresponding to that between first and second torpedoes.

1334. One explosion 1 minute 15 seconds after the second hit. This may have been the first depth charge, or possibly a hit on the tanker, which at the time of firing appeared to be one ship's length astern of the supply ship. The submarine proceeded towards the enemy's stern.

1336. Depth charges dropped singly. This was followed by a pair of depth charges, and then another single one at about two minute intervals. The counter-attack was carried out by one T.B. using asdic. A pattern of ten, dropping fairly close, shook the submarine, causing no damage.

1406. T.B.'s screw heard passing overhead very slowly.

1406½. A pattern of twelve charges dropped close, causing showers of cork, though little real damage beyond lights being smashed and a few small leaks. It is considered that this pattern was dropped slightly on the port quarter and was fortunately set too shallow. After this the pattern became more distant, but no matter what alterations of course were made, the enemy could not be shaken off.

1700 app. Another T.B. joined in the hunt, but seemed to hinder rather than help his expert consort, as only three charges were dropped after this time.

1830 app. H.E. [hydrophone effects] had ceased. 62 charges had been dropped in this counter-attack.

2008. Surfaced. Withdrew to N.E., subsequently setting course to proceed to Malta, all torpedoes being expended.

In such simple words was a page of submarine history recorded. What was its most revealing phrase?—"Fortunately set too shallow." If that pattern dropped at 1406½ had been set deeper Simpson would probably never have read any of these words. The log would have broken off at 1406. As it was, all went well, and, the success having been confirmed, Simpson endorsed it as a "very valuable patrol, carried out with fine dash and judgment, which cost the enemy two ships full of war supplies."

Yet the narrative of the more memorable episodes in these sixteen months only come to life if enough submarine atmosphere is imbibed to appreciate all the aspects on which depend success or failure, life or death.

The only person who knows what is going on is the commanding officer. His are the eyes which watch the enemy. He passes what he sees to the navigator, who by plotting ranges and bearings, courses and speeds, on the chart gets a geometric—or trigonometric—picture of what is happening overhead. But it is a still-life. Only the captain has the perspective, the colouring; only he can see the symmetry of waves creaming away on either side of the sloping knife-like bows of a destroyer swinging round to ram. He alone sees the whole crew, who turn to him in times of strain, as though to learn what is likely to happen through his eyes.

He may be watched in detail, his every mannerism noted, and from his countenance is construed the shape of things to come in the next minutes. Between rapid glimpses through the periscope the captain will either bite his nails, scratch the back of his neck in concentration, or stand stock-still with hands thrust in pockets, cap pushed back, eyes fixed in an unseeing stare, lips pursed in a soundless whistle. The crew know every mood, every sign.

And there is battle in human terms too. From start to finish of a patrol daylight is a delight unknown to the great majority of the crew. Occasionally the navigator and a look-out may get up for a quick astronomical sight, or the gun's crew will have an airing in a few minutes' hectic excitement. But this cannot be called relaxation, firing at a ship from a surfaced sub. For a crash-dive or a hit on the sub. could leave a gun-crew out in the cold—to death by drowning.

Daylight is seen second-hand through the periscope. Fresh air is limited to the after-dark hours when the sub. feels less naked on the surface than during the day. But even at night they must remain ready to dive instantaneously, for an E-boat is hard to spot in the dark and may be practically on top of the sub. before being seen. So only the officer of the watch and a look-out can be on the bridge. No time to tumble spectators below if the sub. has to do a dive suddenly.

At night the engines are busy charging the batteries and sucking great gusts of reviving air down through the conning-tower for a short spell. Then it is that the comfort of a cigarette, so longed for throughout the day, can be enjoyed.

All ships have their own individual atmosphere. But none so distinctive as a submarine after a few days on patrol. Vitiated air, oil, human bodies, food, disinfectant, battery gas, and a score of others go to compose an indescribable fug familiar only to the true-blue submariner.

The story of fresh air smelling strange may well have originated from an engine-room rating after a whole stifling patrol. No sooner had the sub. been secured to her buoy than the hatch sprang open and a pale, maggoty-coloured face popped up from the casing. He rested his oil-smeared elbows, moved his head round to left then to right, and, taking in the dramatically dazzling Malta with eyes screwed up against unaccustomed sun, said:

"Cool What a funny smell!" And he really meant it.

Uncanny contrasts come not only from light and dark, air fresh and foul, but also from noise: the mechanical din when the engines are running; through the steady hum of the motors, with the low voices of the crew at watch-diving stations; to the dead silence when the hunt for the sub. is on and the motors are stopped. Then, down in the depths, the captain loses his distinction of sight, and it is the hydrophone operator who knows what can be expected. Long before the rest of his shipmates the operator hears the first hints of the enemy's movements. He strains his ears to the delicate instruments. Then a sudden staccato statement:

"Turbines—220 revs.—red four five. Moving to starboard, sir."

"Bearing green one oh, sir. Seems to be steadying."

"Enemy coming in to attack, sir."

Now they can all hear. Silence in the sub. But from outside—somewhere above—an ever-growing rustling, rushing; then—thunderous noise rippling through the water and sounding like an express train getting nearer, nearer. The threshing thud of propeller-blades as a destroyer pulses and pounds overhead.

Then the worst moment of all for those in their steel shells fathoms deep. Had they been found? Were depth-charges on their way down? One U-sub.'s crew actually once heard the click of the release-gear aboard the enemy ship as it passed overhead to lay its eggs. And they lived to tell the tale.

Of the senses which convey fear to the mind when a submarine is being depth-charged hearing is the foremost—hearing coupled with the sight of some strange and unaccountable things that happen before the eyes as charges fall really close. The reeling, shuddering upheaval may only break a few bulbs: on the other hand, pieces can be torn off bulkheads and hurled across the vessel. Once a gigantic electric spark shot from one side of the motor-room to the other for no apparent reason. Then there comes the culminating monstrous metallic clang, clashing on the pressure-hull from all sides of the hunted sub., when a depth-charge has detonated.

The known noise is bad enough, but it is the inexplicable that can be even worse. Submariners accept so many hazards that any extra, mysterious ones seem slightly unfair. The Polish submarine *Sokol* suddenly became stuck in the Gulf of Gabes. She could go neither forward nor back. Each man in the crew knew that this might be the end. Perhaps she would not be able to start again before her air supply gave out. She could only stay submerged for a limited time. After that it would be a slow death.

Then, as she stayed and swayed, a soft velvety rustle encompassed her: a weird, unearthly bottom-of-the-sea sound which was at once identified as an area of thick, dreaded seaweed. It entangled her workings badly. But by repeated heavings, wriggling, pumping, her captain somehow struggled free of this fearful zone and got her back to Malta—with trails of seaweed still hanging intertwined around her propeller.

Sokol survived a hundred such escapades. Another time, as she proceeded on patrol at medium depth and in the mid-Mediterranean far from any known shallows, she was suddenly slowed down again and exactly the same rustle was heard. Once more she got free, but her crew never knew what she had run into on this second occasion. It could not have been seaweed at the depth they were keeping. But what was it? And what made that soft, swishing rustle? This pinpoints one of the fundamental factors of life in a submarine. Although the vessel is always underwater, part of the sea itself, no one aboard can know what goes on just a few inches outside the hull.

Sound can play strange tricks. The crash of a depth-charge is so well known as to be commonplace, and it can be easily explained. But no one can yet say in satis-factory terms what accounts for the 'gravel-throwing' that is sometimes heard after it. Submariners describe it as "a handful of gravel hurled against the pressure-hull" when the noise of the explosion has died down. Some strange by-product of acoustics, perhaps—but what?

Few noises are more spine-chilling than the scratchy scraping of a mine wire moving slowly abaft the sub. A disembodied action sounding so near—as, indeed, it is. But supremely sinister of all sounds to shatter the nerves of the 10th Flotilla was the noise of an explosive sweep wire fingering its fiendish way gently over the hull. Here is terror—yet the submariner never shows it, so close to death is he in a dozen different ways. Never can a patrol be commonplace even in peace, far less in war. However routine the operation, there are the crew, always standing silent in their sweaty, smelling prison, where any moment of the day or night may mark the come-back of a counter-attack.

This was life all the year round in 1941.

Full of enthusiasm, keen for a kill, Cayley's crew trooped aboard *Utmost* to leave Malta for another patrol into the unknown. Cayley called them together and explained where they were bound and, as far as he could, what to expect. But no one ever knew really: uncertainty was the only sure thing. There might be mines, nets, patrol vessels, aircraft, depth-charges, bombs—any or all, or none at all.

On this patrol the inexplicable appeared again. And, however harmless it might seem afterwards, and loudly as it might be laughed at, while it is still unknown it remains a strain on the commanding officer responsible for the lives of his crew.

The cool Cayley, resolute as ever, had harried the enemy successfully in *Utmost*, so was not to be troubled by trifles.

Utmost had moved many times in the waters between Malta and Cape Bon. They were mineable, and actually mined in places. The area was, for the most part, shallow with deep channels between Pantelleria and the

Tunisian coast. Ships had been mined in widely separated spots, mostly where the water was shallow, and the whole locality was looked on askance by British submarines. But as the sub. can move in three dimensions— instead of the surface ship's two—it remained an operational risk for subs. to use the deeper water when going about their business down south.

Cayley was well versed in this procedure, but always kept the danger of mines in his mind wherever he went. And on this patrol he was setting off—not south but on his first sally north of Sicily. He was ordered *via* the route which had been used without incident by other submarines many times previously. In the middle of the route Cayley decided to have a routine look around.

"Periscope depth." Then "Up periscope." And in clear calm weather the sub.'s eye broke surface. Cayley made a quick revolution round the horizon—not a sign of ships. A careful search of the sky, after his first rapid glance, told him that no aircraft were about. And again Cayley switched back to the sea.

Suddenly off the starboard bow he saw a half-hidden round black object, undoubtedly a floating mine. Knowing exactly where it was, Cayley had no need to worry unduly. Nor did he—until he saw a second one, dead ahead. Then a third appeared off the port bow, then two more to starboard, then four to port. Before giving the order to alter course he glanced quickly astern. There, to his horror, were other mines bobbing slightly astern and on either quarter. *Utmost* was apparently surrounded by floating mines.

"How the hell did they get there?" Cayley asked. A few moments earlier *Utmost*'s periscope had been the only object visible in the whole wide ocean. "Perhaps it's some new device that makes mines pop up when a ship or a sub. comes along."

It was not surprising that "Harmonica Dick" Cayley began to be anxious. He could not possibly tell how extensive this mysterious minefield might be—nor whether it would be better to go on or back. They seemed to be all around *Utmost*.

"Might as well be hung for a——"

Then, just as he was examining the nearest black 'mine' as calmly as he could, he almost yelled with relief. A stubby head with an evil eye poked out of the mass—and a turtle drifted dozily past the periscope. The warm sun and calm sea, plus a lack of activity among humans afloat, had brought a large school of the turtles to the surface to bask in the Mediterranean.

On the way from the 'minefield' Caley said: "The thought of sitting down with city aldermen to turtle soup no longer appeals to me, chaps! I'd always think of that little lot!"

But the next time that mines were mentioned to Cayley they were real enough and not mock turtles. A large rectangular patch of sea extending right across the channel between Pantelleria and Sicily had been openly declared as a mined area by the Italians, and two Greek ships became casualties in the early days of their country's neutrality. Actual observation on patrol had shown that the previous routes between Pantelleria and Cape Bon were daily becoming too dangerous to be practicable.

"Unless another route can be found, patrols north of Sicily will have to stop, as far as the 10th Submarine Flotilla is concerned," Shrimp Simpson told Cayley, Wanklyn, and Tomkinson, luckily all ashore at the same time. "Now, I've called you three characters together to tell you that it will be essential for me to send three subs. to this area. We've got to find a way through the mines somehow."

Wanklyn's eyes were alight. Cayley rubbed his hands. Tommo stood up to his full stature and smacked his lips.

Simpson went on: "A route north to Pantelleria, through this declared area"—pointing to a wall map— "that seems to be the lesser of the two evils."

The four of them and Tanner pored over a bigger chart and discussed exactly which would be the best route. At last they decided on the detail to be followed.

"I don't like asking you to do this at all, really," Simpson apologized; "but at least they can't have mined the whole rectangle—and at all depths. Nevertheless, I want you to know that I'm not pleased at having to order the submarines through."

Then came a moment's silence—for, although the three commanding officers had been joking with their captain and the staff officer, all five of them knew that the mission might prove fatal to one of the subs. And they were all aware that one more decision still had to be taken.

"Well, that's that. The only other thing to settle is who'll go first."

"I will, sir," said Cayley, without a second's pause. Wanklyn and Tomkinson were already about to say so too.

But Cayley had been too quick for them. The others were ordered on no account to proceed until Cayley sent a signal saying that he was through the mines and well clear of land. He took *Utmost* out as calmly as if the sub. were on a day's exercise in the Channel from *Dolphin* or Weymouth.

So the three subs. left for the area. *Urge* and *Upholder* lagged a long way behind, as they were to follow at twenty-four-hour intervals.

Cayley crept along blind, relying entirely on soundings and dead reckoning to keep him on the prescribed track. Back at base, in the Operations Room of Lazaretto, the staff anxiously awaited a signal to tell them all was well. If it were not, and *Utmost* met a mine, they would only be able to assume so through the silence. For a mine might flood the sub. in a second or two and drown the whole crew.

"We've been lucky so far," Simpson told Tanner; "let's hope it holds. But I suppose sooner or later we'll have to face the fact of one or more going."

The clock crept round as slowly as Cayley was advancing. The slower the sub. went the better, for the less sound she would make to attract the attention of any acoustic mines—the latest Axis weapon. The atmosphere in the Ops. Room got tense, tight-strung, tauter. Simpson grew silent. Then a signal came:

"Next, please!"

The captain breathed a long, long sigh, as if he had not exhaled for hours. As far as he remembered, he had not.

Aboard *Utmost*, Cayley fingered his harmonica. As he came up to surface that night, a still moonlit Mediterranean dusk with magic in the Sicilian Sea, Cayley thrust a hand into his pocket, brought out the beloved mouth-organ, moistened his lips—still dry from the long ordeal earlier—and blew a little trill of triumph.

"Glad that's over," he confided to his Number One.

H

Utmost was followed by *Urge* and *Upholder*. Each arrived safely in the Tyrrhenian Sea and returned the same way without meeting any mines or ships. But it was Cayley who had blazed the way first.

Back at Malta, three glasses clinked in the mess.

"To Daredevil Dick," the other two teased. His harmonica was still safe in his jacket pocket.

After Cayley's sustained spring effort of forty out of sixty days at sea *Utmost* carried out eight patrols in the difficult and dangerous early summer. Two ships were sunk in six attacks.

And a mercy mission too was added to Cayley's list of assignments. Malta received an SOS signal by radio from a damaged Blenheim aircraft. "Losing height rapidly," followed by the plane's position, 145 miles from the island.

Simpson routed *Utmost* to the spot as soon as possible. The sub. was only a few miles off at the time, patrolling to the north of Tripoli.

Cayley came to periscope depth. "Can't see a thing —we'll have to surface."

"In daylight, sir?" a junior asked.

"Yes. There are R.A.F. chaps somewhere in the sea, and they may be dying, for all we know. We've got to find them—quickly."

So *Utmost* surfaced in the strong sun, a sitting target to any enemy aircraft. She sailed slowly around the area. Then the look-out suddenly shouted.

"There they are!" A group of exhausted airmen lay huddled in a dinghy a mile or more away. In a quarter of an hour the sub. was alongside, and ten minutes later they were all down in bunks sipping tots of rum.

Another encounter in the mine-infested area south of

Pantelleria rivalled Cayley's turtles. "Jock" Mackenzie was keeping *Ursula* deep as much as possible, since hydrophone listening conditions were good for any enemy about above. Before he had taken her down deep the island of Sicily had still been in sight and the sea glassy calm. Then the 'secret weapon' asserted itself.

"Propeller noises starboard, sir," said the sub.'s hydrophone operator suddenly.

"Bearing and range?" queried Mackenzie.

"Long way off, sir. Very faint. Sounds like motor-boat engines. Bearing about green one oh, sir."

"Periscope depth," the skipper said.

He watched the depth-gauge intently, then signalled for the periscope to be raised as he trained it to ten degrees starboard—the translation of green one oh.

"Bearing now?"

"Green one three, sir."

Mackenzie trained on to this new bearing and cautiously started to raise the periscope the last few inches.

He saw the still blue water fading lighter and lighter: from Mediterranean blue, through pale green, to white. It stirred from utter stillness to a mass of movement, as air bubbles near the surface burst and flashed past the periscope. As always, he was fascinated looking from the lower end to the upper, many feet above. Slowly it poked its way up from the gloom to the bright world of water and sun on the surface. From stillness to motion. What would he see? And where?

Mackenzie confidently expected to sight a low, indistinct outline, oscillating in the distance, of an Italian M.A.S. cruising far out on his starboard bow—with the grey-blue hump of Pantelleria breaking the horizon.

The upper glass broke surface. For a second all seemed scintillating as silver sprayed, shimmered, broke, and ran down the sloping window. Then a dark, blurred image slowly took shape in the strong sun—the shape of a horrible, horned mine that twisted, turned, and bobbed up and down only a few yards from Mackenzie's gaze. But it did not pop as much as Jock's eyes at the sight of it up there large as life.

"Can you really hear something, operator?" he asked urgently.

"Yessir! Motor-boat. Fast, and getting louder. Same bearing, sir."

"Well, some one's crackers. There's a floating mine on that bearing and it ain't moving! And, anyway, mines don't make noises like motor-boats. Or do they? Here, Number One—have a quick look while I listen."

The first lieutenant confirmed the mine. Mackenzie clamped on the earphones and caught the unmistakable acoustics of a fast-moving motor-boat. He hurried back to the periscope. This was all happening in seconds. He was only a step from the hydrophones. He thought quickly of the possibility of a secret weapon in the form of a clockwork mine of some sort. Could that make the noise?

The control-room leapt into action as he rapped out:

"Hard to port. Flood Q. Eighty feet. Quick!"

Ursula sank like a stone as every one aboard heard a fast ship threshing through the water directly overhead.

"What happened?" Number One asked, when they were relatively safe at a decent depth.

"The mine filled the whole field," Mackenzie explained. "It blotted out an M.A.S. completely. The boat must have been coming to investigate it."

Fortunately, Mackenzie thought with split-second speed. The dramatic appearance round the side of the sphere of a curving bow-wave and then the sharp flaring bows had stung him into instant reaction—and the quickest dive he ever did.

One day in '41 *Upright's* crew must have felt certain that they would meet disaster. Under "Johnny" Wraith's command, they were proceeding at periscope depth to cross the hundred-fathom line. Suddenly two heavy bumps were heard—and a scraping sound down the ship's side. Nothing could be seen astern through the periscope.

"Must be a mine," Johnny said.

They altered course quickly to the northward, and *Upright* kept outside the hundred-fathom line for the rest of the patrol. The deeper the water the safer the sub. —a good motto as far as evasive action for mines went.

Summer 1941 saw many such perils. Tomkinson fired a full salvo of four at a convoy; but one torpedo stuck half-way out of its tube, the weapon's engine running all the while. *Urge* had to come swiftly to the surface brandishing an angry, smoking torpedo at the foe! Tommo was livid as he looked through the periscope at the start of the attack to find his view for'ard totally blotted out by smoke and steam. All he could see were the sharp bows of the submarine.

"Who ordered a blessed smokescreen?" he roared.

But as *Urge* levelled off on the surface a clever combination of her swinging under helm, the judicious rattling of the torpedo's operating gear, and the prayers and oaths of all aboard resulted in the offending weapon leaving its tube. The torpedo gunner's mate swore softly to himself and then raised his eyes in a fleeting prayer as the thing sped on its way. *Urge* put on full steam and somehow managed to duck herself down again at a very steep angle.

All this occurred in broad daylight before the astonished gaze of the enemy. Just as *Urge* dived Tommo got a glimpse of the nearest escort, a mere 3000 yards off during this unrehearsed performance. It turned towards the sub., and the only possible explanation for her failing to open fire was that her crew must have been as staggered as the submariners at what was going on. The whole fantastic feat took only a couple of minutes, and before *Urge* went into her steep descent to the depths they heard three torpedo hits. One of them Tomkinson actually saw on a large supply-ship beyond the escort that had been bearing down on them. This trio of hits— a maximum possible in view of the fourth's failure— were ample compensation for those hundred or so seconds on the surface.

Twenty depth-charges, broadcast in somewhat haphazard style, did not come very close, and *Urge* continued her patrol, ignoring the wayward behaviour of the fourth torpedo in the salvo. It could have been deadly dangerous, though, if it had not left the tube.

As if this were not enough for one patrol, she subsequently sank a large transport before returning again to Malta.

Throughout the summer the Italians made every effort to reinforce the African armies, and it was gradually becoming easier to locate their convoys. But submarine tactics were complicated by the short distance of the run from Italy to Tripoli: little more than 400 miles from Palermo and about 500 from Naples. Moreover, the enemy could afford to employ heavy escorts for a small number of supply-ships. The convoys now consisted of some four ships, escorted by three to five destroyers or torpedo-boats.

Tomkinson and Wanklyn were both enjoying great success. On *Upholder*'s tenth patrol she sank the 6000-ton *Laura C*, a supply-ship, and survived nineteen depth-charges.

Another supply-ship went down on the next patrol, and she probably sank in the same sortie a Condottiere-class cruiser travelling at high speed, with a second cruiser and two destroyers accompanying her. The higher the speed the harder to hit.

Upholder could not wait for Wanklyn to see, as thirty depth-charges clattered and crashed towards the seabed where she lay.

Loud, then louder, sounded the ship's screws. Then came the great metallic clang—the 'tonk,' as they called it. *Upholder*'s shell shuddered. The white paint corking fell in a showering spray over the mess. Depth-gauges were splintered. Glass broke, and clattered on to the deck. Another tonk, and another. An empty teacup jumped two feet into the air from the mess-table—and then shattered.

Patrol number twelve brought more bags: a supply-ship and a tanker sunk, and a hit on a 6-inch cruiser. The tanker exploded in a darkening cloud of black belching smoke from burning fuel. The day of doom looked at hand. Then the ship sank, and the great pall still hung on the horizon.

But *Upholder* saw nothing. An accurate attack came from three escorting destroyers. They tore to the area where the attack had been launched. The Mediterranean was lashed and churned on either side of their three bows—and they dropped singles and patterns of depth-charges until there were aching heads in *Upholder*. By Wanklyn's usual incomparable seamanship the sub. dodged her record number of depth-charges—sixty in the single counter-attack.

The thirteenth patrol was unlucky. Nothing to report.

But Wanklyn's work was beginning to bear the mark of the master, a relentless inevitability, effected by a wonderfully clear conception of strategy, a mind enabling him to assess ships' movements and intentions, and by letting other people get on with their own jobs without interference. Anyone could go to him in trouble, but *he* rarely worried *them*.

Now it was a success with almost every sortie. On his next patrol he was to crown his career with an operation of startling brilliance. But first came the incomparable Commander Karnicki and the start of the *Sokol* story.

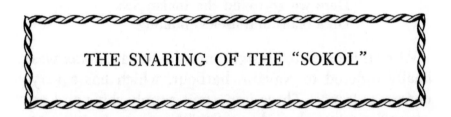

11

THE SNARING OF THE "SOKOL"

THE snaring of the *Sokol* was one of the strangest of many harbour adventures experienced by Allied submarines anywhere in the Mediterranean. This proud Polish sub. had joined the Malta force eagerly, and at once showed her spirit, even before the snaring story.

Her captain, Lieutenant-Commander Boris Karnicki, had served with submarines since the day Germany pillaged Poland—September 1, 1939. And on *Sokol*'s very first patrol he attacked a heavily escorted convoy northwest of Naples. She hit and damaged the auxiliary motor-cruiser *Citta di Palermo*.

Then, while returning to Malta at night, she encountered a north-bound enemy merchantman. Karnicki started to attack with torpedoes, but the night was dark and, not surprisingly, they missed their mark. But he was not beaten. Going in on the surface, he took *Sokol* straight for the enemy, with the sub.'s little 12-pounder gun at the ready, and fired from the fantastic range of fifty yards—and sank her.

So to the snaring. On his second outing Karnicki patrolled with four of the U-class vessels. These unfortunate five submarines found themselves sent to so many

different positions at short intervals that the operation
gave birth to fresh lyrics of the "Mulberry Bush":

> Here we go round the Ionian Sea,
> Ionian Sea, Ionian Sea;
> Here we go round the Ionian Sea,
> On a blank and useless hunting.

After this extended insight into the Ionian, *Sokol* was
finally ordered to Navarin harbour, which has a very
narrow entrance. Three important supply-ships and an
escort lay at anchor there. So far as was known, no
obstructions to the entrance existed, and *Sokol* had
complete liberty of action to attack or not, according to
circumstances. Commander Karnicki gave all this intelligence his usual deep thought, and planned a careful
campaign. He made arrangements for the rapid reloading of torpedo tubes, as he hoped to steal into the harbour unseen and sink the convoy, starting with its
escort.

Shortly after dawn *Sokol* was situated three miles off
the entrance, and proceeded according to her commander's plan. Two and a half hours later there followed
the most hectic and harrowing forty-five minutes
possible to imagine.

Less than a mile from the entrance, travelling at very
slow speed, *Sokol* had covered two-thirds of the distance
to the harbour. Then, suddenly she bumped on the
bottom at thirty-eight feet and bounced up to twenty-
eight. This was the prelude. The Polish sailors clutched
at anything handy and reeled down the length of the
submarine.

She descended to forty-three feet and started to
change course to enter the harbour. She rose to peri-

scope depth to check her position and look around. But Commander Karnicki got the glare from the low-lying early-morning sun directly in his line of vision with a vital part of the harbour.

She dived to forty feet and put on speed. Suddenly the sound of wires scraping down the hull meant more trouble. *Sokol* came to a standstill. The jerk made the periscope shudder and flicker wildly to and fro.

A mine exploded. A violent eruption followed, and the sub. jumped two feet. Both motors stopped at once. Tanks flooded. Men scrambled aft to try to keep the stern down. They did not want the sub. seen. She would be sunk in a second.

Sokol was secured in a net.

She plunged wildly about like a trapped animal, and restarted motors. She tried them at full speed astern for five minutes. They must have given her away. The three hundred seconds seemed as many minutes. Then *Sokol* started to move, and with a bouncing, wriggling motion began to drop down. The men were still being flung for'ard and aft. One or two more jerks as her weight wormed out of the net. And in another three minutes she was clear.

At a more comfortable depth of 130 feet they heard two motor-boats overhead. But she escaped detection, after all that noise. Miraculously nothing else happened, so *Sokol* could creep away undisturbed. Soon to return.

Commander Karnicki surveyed his damage dolefully, and the sub. licked her wounds. The encounter with the anti-submarine net cost her a flooded periscope and a damaged aerial. To say nothing of somewhat frayed nerves.

That night they received a signal saying that the entrance to the harbour was believed to be strongly defended by nets and mines!

"Is this the English sense of humour we 'ear so much about?" the commander asked with a chuckle. But he was a persistent and patient Pole—as well as being impetuous on occasion. He had made up his mind to carry out this attack, come mines or menaces of any sort, so he remained on patrol off the harbour entrance to wait for the ships to set sail. In the early morning he focused his periscope on the inside of the harbour and could see two destroyers there, but no other ships—although he saw smoke rising from behind the hills. An air-raid, or a reconnaissance, prompted the destroyers and local shore batteries to open fire spiritedly, and Commander Karnicki noticed that the larger destroyer looked very vulnerable to attack from outside the harbour itself.

He closed to the harbour entrance at ultra-slow speed. Suddenly one of the other officers pointed out that Poland was not at war with Italy! Karnicki paused and frowned for a second, then said:

"I hereby declare war on Benito Mussolini!"

Then, with nice calculation and endearing impudence, he fired three torpedoes through the hole that *Sokol* had made in the anti-sub. net! He immediately altered course, as by now they were dangerously near to the net. One torpedo ran amok. He watched aghast as its track bubbled across the submarine's bows just in front of his periscope. But eventually, though, it headed in the right direction without hitting anything.

The second and third produced undoubted explosions, with the gurgling noises and all the other sounds of a ship breaking up. One debt had been settled, and the crew shook pairs of hands joyfully.

But still the day had not run its course. The commander spotted the second destroyer heading out of the harbour at speed, while seventeen depth-charges shattered the waters within the entrance. *Sokol* dived deep to reload her tubes as the destroyer, and two motorboats observed earlier, ran around and dropped fifty-five further charges.

This counter-attack incensed the Pole, who was now determined to get the supply-ships too, which he knew were there but could not see. And, sure enough, that night the convoy came out. *Sokol* surfaced and turned on full speed. A short chase, and then one of the ships was hit, if not sunk, by two torpedoes.

Commander Karnicki now wears the ribbon of the Distinguished Service Order, alongside those of the Virtuti Militari and the Cross of Valour, two high Polish decorations.

He was not a voluble—or a volatile—type; rather, he would think deeply and bring out really trenchant remarks. And he must have thought quite a bit on the return passage from Navarin to Malta. Describing the patrol to Captain Simpson, he said:

"Captain, it is a bad thing for any submarine to be caught in any net, but it is a special pity for a Polish submarine to be caught in an Italian net. You see, sir, I had no real alternative but to make my declaration of war!"

The return of *Sokol* from this first successful patrol turned out to be quite dramatic. Malta had heard by the Poles' victim's SOS over the air of *Sokol's* success at Navarin. So it occurred to the Operations Room that

Commander Karnicki had no Jolly Roger to fly as he entered harbour. This was by now a classic emblem of a submarine's success on patrol. So a flag was ordered to be put in hand at once—complete with one big bar.

Very early on the morning of her expected arrival date two silent figures scrambled down on to the Malta rocks and sat there staring out to sea. They were two Polish seamen of *Sokol's* spare crew. They had been disappointed because they could not go out on patrol too, and now anxiously awaited their sub.'s return, quite unconcerned that it would be several hours before she hove into sight. Their comrades were coming back successfully and must be met.

Another surprise reception for *Sokol* completed their moment of triumph.

Soon after breakfast Simpson was astonished to hear from Valletta that General Sikorski was returning from a visit to the Near East and happened to be in Malta. Naturally the General wanted to see his submariners. He was delighted to hear of *Sokol's* success and that she would soon be sailing up the creek at Lazaretto.

Commander Karnicki knew nothing of all these preparations for *Sokol's* return.

Simpson strode aboard as *Sokol* secured. He held out his hand to the Pole.

"Congratulations. And we've got a surprise for you. Will you muster your crew on the 'quarter deck' ashore, my dear fellow?"

Half an hour later, spick and span, the Poles were lined up behind their beloved commander.

"Let me introduce the commander to you, General," Simpson said. And the Pole saw for the first time his country's own Prime Minister and Commander-in-Chief.

Simpson primed Sikorski in advance about the signifi-
cance of the Jolly Roger. The General then made a short
speech in their native tongue and presented the grati-
fied commander with the black-and-white flag, bearing
its new bar.

The normally imperturbable crew could not conceal
their feelings when Karnicki called for three cheers for
their C.-in-C. Round the courtyard rang three weird,
full-throated Polish cries—a happy, spontaneous
acclamation, which was far better than the careful
planning that usually precedes ceremonial inspec-
tions.

The crew of *Sokol* was a great company, in the tradition set by her sister submarines *Orzel* and *Wilk*. They
had been sent to the Mediterranean, far from the theatre
of war in which they were naturally most interested.
The majority of them had no news of the welfare or
even whereabouts of their families, yet they set out
on patrols with an *élan* and enthusiasm impossible to
outdo.

Patrols always seemed too short for them, and the
time spent in harbour was wasted time as far as they
were concerned if *Sokol* happened to be fit for sea. They
required no rest ashore, they said, and only wanted to
be allowed to get at the enemy as often as possible. They
had the full support of Commander Karnicki and
"George," his second-in-command. On one occasion
Sokol was destined to be in dock having her bottom
scraped and painted, an essential maintenance. It
seemed uncertain whether she could be refloated in time
to participate in plans to intercept a certain convoy, so
she was excluded from the arrangements as "not available." But Karnicki came close to tears when he heard

of it. And after much discussion, persuasion, and pleading Captain Simpson at last relented.

"All right, you can go along too—but only if *Sokol*'s ready by the time the others are due to leave. We just can't put the patrol back even an hour. I would if I could."

Then more powers of persuasion were brought to bear on the crew, and *Sokol* managed to make it—with five minutes to spare!

A wealth of humour lay behind Commander Karnicki's deep-set eyes, but he was slightly bewildered at times by the notorious vagaries of the English language. He took genuine delight in recounting his latest *faux pas*. One of the most amusing occurred at the end of a party at a house in Malta. After thoroughly enjoying himself he went up to thank his hostess for the enchanting evening. He had prepared his phrase in advance—for safety, as he thought. When taking his leave he astounded the lady by making a formal Polish bow over her outstretched hand and saying in all solemnity:

"God pickle you, madam!"

"You see," he explained subsequently to Shrimp Simpson shaking with joy, "my English was not so good then. I wanted to say the right thing. In Poland we say 'God preserve you.' So what do I do? I look in the dictionary for the word and I find 'to pickle or preserve.' So I say 'God pickle you.'"

Simpson had the last laugh, though.

"I reckon it was you who were pickled, my friend!"

"Pardon?"

"Never mind. Pickled has another slang meaning too, you know. It means being merry, or drunk."

"Ah, I see. Well, let's say I was partly pickled."

The comforting aspect was that Karnicki's hostess had received his genuine if unorthodox expression of cordiality with true traditional British calm!

I

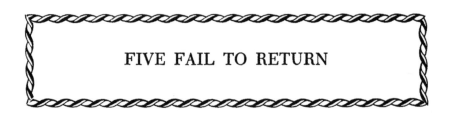

12

FIVE FAIL TO RETURN

INDIRECTLY concerned with the 10th Flotilla's movements, another operation involving the island came to be called the "Magic Carpet Service to Malta." This was a remarkable institution of the 1st Flotilla, based on Alexandria. The larger P-class submarines operating in the eastern end of the Mediterranean were used to carry vital supplies to the island. The *Porpoise* came first. She embarked a cargo of petrol and mines—not the best of bed-fellows under the ocean—and also carried out a minelaying operation on the way just for good measure. She made nine trips to Malta altogether as an underwater freighter, and with other subs. maintained a supply of aviation spirit, which helped the Fleet Air Arm and R.A.F. to keep flying.

During July this Magic Carpet Service conveyed to Malta 126 passengers, 84,280 gallons of petrol, 83,340 gallons of kerosene, twelve tons of mail, thirty tons of general stores, and six tons of munitions, including torpedoes for the U-class submarines and the few aircraft which could carry them.

A suitable design for the house-flag of the "Malta Shipping Company" came into creation, too. An unspectacular but hazardous job without which Malta could not have carried on with her war. How the island got her supplies remained a mystery to Germans and Italians alike. In fact, the whole operation was conducted on the wonderful Magic Carpet—but underwater instead of in the sky.

This was the safe way to supply the island. The surface route right through from Gibraltar was widely exposed to the enemy; and we just did not have the aircraft to act as freighters.

While this service survived without loss, the months on patrol began to take their toll of the little force of Malta subs. In April 1941 the last signal was received from *Usk*, operating in the Marittimo area. On May 1 *Undaunted* transmitted her final message from the Tripoli zone; and on her very first patrol. *Union* never returned from a July patrol to Pantelleria.

One day late in August Simpson strode restlessly about the Ops. Room. For once his face showed the strain he was suffering.

"P33 a day overdue, Geoffrey—and now P32."

"They may turn up, sir."

But they both knew that P33 had only a thousand-to-one chance now.

A duty rating put up the black-out in the room. Another rating tapped on the door at dawn to take it down. Stale smoke, red-rimmed eyes, silent resignation.

Meanwhile, Hezlet had assumed command of *Unique* to give Collett a rest in reward for his good work. *Unique* sailed on August 14 with orders to patrol in a position north of Tripoli, eight miles from P33 and twelve miles from P32. All three subs. were disposed to intercept a slow convoy approaching Tripoli. *Unique* was told to establish contact with both P-class subs. on the 18th. But she could not get through to P33, and by the 20th knew that the sub. might be lost. W.T. signals from Malta confirmed the situation. Hezlet spoke to P32 on the 18th, but by the 20th this sub. too failed to respond.

Hezlet knew only too well that the area must be highly hazardous. At 1000 hours on the 20th, ten miles west-north-west of Tripoli, Hezlet suddenly sighted a fast convoy of four south-bound liners escorted by three flying-boats. He did not hesitate. He launched a skilful, sure attack with the thought of P32 and P33 bursting his brain. From 700 yards *Unique* got three hits on s.s. *Esperia* of 11,300 tons. She sank. Hezlet reported back to base of the success—and continued absence of the two subs.

Simpson sent another sub. to the Tripoli area to search exhaustively for the final time. Even at war we remembered men. The subs. were vital too—but it was the men who mattered most.

The signal came through during the next day:

"No trace of either."

Shrimp Simpson swallowed.

"That's five."

"Yes, sir."

Each one was a wound to them.

Through the summer, too, the submarines undertook a series of other offensive operations, in addition to the perpetual patrols. These were landings conducted by troops carried offshore by the subs. Once ashore, they did as much damage as they could in the shortest space of time before re-embarking.

First Tomkinson took *Urge* towards Taormina, where Wanklyn had spent part of his honeymoon. On the night of June 26–27 he landed a military party four miles north of the town. They crept along in the middle of the night to the entrance of a railway tunnel and laid a charge on the track. Then the blackened men clambered up the rail embankment and withdrew before dawn to the safety of the sub. Across the moonlit beach they ran, and away in their canoes. And as they paddled out to sea the sound of a train came over the air. It chugged through the tunnel and then, as it reached the far end, there came the shattering explosion of it being blown to bits.

Later, air reconnaissance showed that this blocked all East Sicilian rail traffic for some time afterwards.

The next month parties landed from *Unique* on successive nights and destroyed at least one more train.

And then Cayley, commanding *Utmost*, took troops on five separate occasions. They blew up a train, damaged a bridge, and demolished a length of rail.

13

WANKLYN'S FINEST HOUR

By September five of the submarines had been sunk, and five more were still to be lost. But the enemy fared far worse. Then came Wanklyn's wonderful fourteenth patrol.

The late summer saw the crystallization of different tactics. Simpson had got to know the enemy's routes really well. They were having to limit the use of North African ports to Benghazi and Tripoli for large convoys. Their battleship forces also had to make more frequent sorties, because of the growing losses to the convoys inflicted by both submarine and air attack.

These losses prompted the Commander-in-Chief, Mediterranean, to send the following message to Simpson in the summer:

"I wish to congratulate you and your command on the excellent results which have been obtained against the Tripoli convoys in the last few months. Your work is invaluable to the Empire's effort and more than ever important in the present difficult times. Keep it up."

And, to do so, Simpson switched tactics.

Up till then, submarines had usually worked independently, each in a prearranged area. But whenever circumstances allowed the new strategy was for three or even more subs. to operate together on a line athwart the enemy's expected route. Only now, of course, did Simpson begin to get enough vessels to contemplate such strategy. With the few he had originally, one combined patrol would have been more than he could muster. For while three subs. were out at sea, at least as many would be at Malta between patrols so that the crew could rest and the submarine be serviced.

This group operation gave rise to a new term in Lazaretto. 'Banana peeler' meant the submarine in the billet nearest to the direction the enemy were expected. If this first sub. were fortunate enough to get into a position possible for an attack she invariably received the full fury of the counter-attack, which was as often as not fairly spent in terms of depth-charges by the time enemy escorts reached other submarines in the line. The last in line, therefore, had an exceptionally easy time, but he might never get a run for his money if there were no convoy left, or if it had found things too hot and had turned back.

No; 'banana peeling' was no plum!

Nicely plotted out on the chart in theory, this principle of three or four subs. in line looked pretty good. The enemy would have to make a very wide sweep to avoid all of them. But in practice, as Simpson was sensible enough to realize it would, the principle failed on a remarkable and infuriating number of occasions. Time after time the submarine patrol lines were strung across the Gulf of Taranto. Equally often battleships came out of the harbour. And, equally often, they slipped past the subs. unscathed. Sometimes the subs.

did not sight the enemy; at other times they did; but always an attack seemed to prove impossible.

But just as Simpson was beginning to despair of ever being lucky the 'Neptunia and Oceania' patrol restored his faith. Everything went with a precision remarkable in the expanse of the Mediterranean.

In August it became apparent that activities farther to the eastward were forcing the enemy to make more use of Tripoli as their main port of disembarkation for materials—and men.

About the middle of September our reconnaissance aircraft spotted three large liners at Taranto.

Unbeaten, Upholder, Upright, and *Ursula* were brought to short notice—and sailed as soon as they could, to a preconceived plan. About a fortnight earlier two troop-transports reached Tripoli despite air and submarine dispositions to stop them. They had been under almost continuous air reconnaissance and a large proportion of their route established. Intelligent guess-work filled in the gaps. And it seemed a safe bet that, as they had arrived actually unmolested, their successors would repeat the route. So Simpson laid his plans.

As soon as the four subs. got the word that the enemy liners had sailed, given from a reccy plane and relayed from Malta H.Q. to Lazaretto, three of them took up a line at an angle across the enemy's route to the north of Misurata, on the north-west corner of the Gulf of Sirte. They were positioned in the hope that one, two, or all three of them would be able to attack in the dark just before dawn. The fourth sub., *Ursula*, having six torpedo tubes, fielded at 'long stop' several miles to the west, where she would be able to attack during daylight in any desired direction. So complete was the coverage by reconnaissance aircraft that the subs. had time to leave Malta and reach their positions leisurely several hours before the enemy's estimated time of arrival.

The weather was good, the trap set. So cut and dried did it all appear that Commander Tanner (he had just been promoted) turned into his bunk at Lazaretto, sure that the telephone on the little table at his side would waken him about 0400 with news from the cypher office. It did.

But meanwhile, by sunset, *Unbeaten*, *Upholder*, and *Upright* all reached their required positions. They had orders to maintain relative positions, keeping a specified distance apart, with *Upholder* in the centre as datum point. When the enemy was sighted, or a report of the enemy received, they could then act on their own. The three craft checked and adjusted their distances before dark, and settled down to a night of patrolling as a unit.

Early on, however, *Upholder* suffered a severe setback, which would have knocked off balance a commanding officer less gifted than Wanklyn. The sub.'s gyro-compass ceased to function altogether, leaving him to rely solely on the much less accurate magnetic compass. This substitute had a wildly swinging card, which put precise steering out of the question, and increased the difficulties of attack a hundredfold.

0320. Woodward in *Unbeaten* sighted the convoy to the north, steaming too fast for him to close in time. He made an immediate report to the others. He had no doubt that Wanklyn would attack, so Woodward whipped *Unbeaten* off westward in the hope of being able to pick up any lame ducks after *Upholder* had finished.

Wanklyn received Woodward's report, and had little
to do but count off the minutes till the enemy came in
sight. Not that the whole thing would be as automatic
as that. The night still stayed dark—ideal for an attack
on the surface. All four subs. were surfaced, waiting.

What were they waiting for? The *Neptunia, Oceania,*
and *Vulcania,* three very valuable liners acting as fully
laden troop-carriers. These converted liners represented
nearly 60,000 tons.

Six destroyers escorted the three transports.

Tubby Crawford was on watch when *Upholder*
sighted them. In a flash Wanklyn was on the bridge.
Together they saw dimly the dark shapes against a dark
horizon to the north-east. An eerie, exciting moment.
The sea was choppy now. Wanklyn realized that the
sub. was some way off the enemy's track. He closed at
full throttle. One small sub. versus nine heavy enemy
ships. The other subs. were still out of range.

With torpedo tubes at the ready, and his glasses glued
to the murky masses on the starboard bow, Wanklyn
raced in to try to intercept the three monsters. He
penetrated the ring of escorting destroyers with con-
summate skill, but realized that he would have to carry
out the attack at a far longer range than he would wish.
The enemy's course could only be gauged to the nearest
mile or so. Most serious of all, *Upholder* was 'yawing'
wildly. Despite the helmsman's efforts to guess what the
compass-card would do next, steering by the magnetic
compass on the surface of a choppy sea was hopelessly
inaccurate. It would have been a waste to fire a salvo of
four under these conditions—for if Wanklyn were wrong
once, through no fault of his own, the one vital opportunity would be over.

He drove on and on, weighing up his chances every second or so. When Wanklyn knew he could not get nearer than 5000 yards he decided finally to fire. Over his cream sweater, an old uniform jacket with wisps of gold braid flaking from the sleeves and several rips around the side under the arms. He did not mind.

Upholder still swung from side to side as the helmsman had to correct the course almost each moment.

"Never get on the line of fire," Wanklyn shouted above the elements.

So, as the sub. swung from one side of the target to the other, he made split-second assessments. Through the glasses in the before-dawn dark he could just see *Oceania* in the lead with *Neptunia* overlapping along the line from the sub.

Upholder swung across the line—and Wanklyn fired.

She swung back again across it, and he fired again. And a few seconds later, as she came on course for the third successive time, he fired once more. Each was judged entirely by eye in the gloom of 4 A.M. Five thousand yards they had to travel, on a dark choppy night with aiming almost impossible. Nearly three miles of black sea. . . .

"Ready to dive, sir?" Crawford called up to Wanklyn. The first lieutenant had gone below when the captain took over to attack.

"Not quite, Tubby," came the reassuring Scots voice. "I want to see them hit first!"

"You'd be better down here, sir!"

In the end Crawford had to clamber aloft and persuade him it was high time to be diving. So she dived quickly and moved to the south.

Back at base, the Ops. Room received the report that

Upholder had sighted the enemy. Now Simpson and Tanner were waiting again—as usual. The three torpedoes took over three minutes to reach the target area, so long was the range. Then as *Upholder* gained depth —50, 60, 80, 100 feet—Wanklyn's watch became the focus. At the precise times planned—they heard two deep bangs.

But in fact he had got one hit on the *Oceania* and two on *Neptunia*. The score was three out of three: a truly amazing achievement in the adverse circumstances— darkness, compass out of action, three-mile range, and choppy sea.

What happened next is learned from an Italian soldier's diary describing those frantic few minutes before dawn. He had been travelling aboard the *Oceania* and was later rescued in the water. Then, months afterwards, he became a prisoner in the Western Desert. The story of the other ships he got from his comrades in the rest of the convoy, who were also saved from the sea.

Several alarms worried them after the convoy left Taranto, but by this near-dawn before reaching Tripoli they were hopeful of docking without disaster—like the previous convoy.

When, without warning, a torpedo tore into *Oceania's* propellers. She was in no danger of sinking, so two destroyers dashed in to try to get her in tow. But exactly as they did so the other two torpedoes dug deep into *Neptunia* amidships. Their two explosions—which Wanklyn took to be one—crippled her. Soon it was sure she would sink. But she could crawl along at about five knots—with a list increasing each minute.

The third of the transport trio, *Vulcania*, collected

one of the destroyers and fled for Tripoli at a phenomenal speed.

Back at Malta, they had hopes of *Ursula,* at long stop,
catching *Vulcania.*

Obviously it was only a matter of minutes for *Neptunia.* Finally she limped and listed to a stop—and sank.
Pandemonium reigned as soldiers slid off the decks into
the sea. The destroyers around her steamed in to collect
survivors and then swung back to *Oceania.*

Wanklyn, however, knew nothing of this. The unaccustomed absence of any counter-attack satisfied him
that the destroyers were too busy searching for survivors
to worry about hunting *Upholder.* And while anyone
remained alive in the water, of course, they could not
drop depth-charges. Wanklyn tried to get in touch with
Woodward of *Unbeaten* for help in completing the con-
quest. But he couldn't raise a reply.

0445. "Stand by to surface."

Then to Crawford: "I'm going up to survey the situation." He could not resist it any longer.

Slowly, splashing as little as he could, Wanklyn
brought the sub. up—among the enemy destroyers. It
was still dark, but a ghostly glimmer from the east lit
enough for him to see one ship stopped, with a destroyer
standing by, another making to westward, also with a
destroyer; and no sign of the third. He left *Upright* and
Ursula to deal with the wounded bird—which was
Neptunia and sank of its own accord. Wanklyn concentrated on the stationary *Oceania.*

He took *Upholder* down again and made off to the
eastward while reloading his tubes, to get a good
position up-sun from which to attack after sunrise.

0630. The sun blazed just above the horizon.

Upholder came up to periscope depth and approached the *Oceania* and her attendant destroyer. Both boats lay stopped but drifting slowly south-east.

Wanklyn got *Oceania* in his sight, and the periscope picked its way slowly nearer, nearer, to the transport. He was just going to fire when he shouted:

"Good God. Forty-five feet."

He had suddenly sighted a second destroyer bows-on only one hundred yards off. Undeterred, Wanklyn took *Upholder* along at forty-five feet, and ducked directly underneath the escort! Then, realizing that this delay and the drift of the target would bring *Upholder* much too close to the escort to fire, he altered depth again.

"Eighty feet."

And *Upholder* went on under the transport too, so as to come up to windward. This was a brilliant bit of manœuvring. Wanklyn looked through his periscope next at an ideal range of 2000 yards from *Oceania*. He fired two torpedoes through the mile and more of water. Both hit, and the ship sank in eight minutes. Thus Wanklyn, alone and unaided, had disposed of two-thirds of this vitally valuable convoy: he had sunk two nearly 20,000-ton transports.

And while Wanklyn was making the final kill of *Oceania*, an amazed man, Lieutenant Woodward, was peering through *Unbeaten*'s periscope not far away. Although Woodward had never received Wanklyn's call for help, *Unbeaten* was already anticipating the need and moving over towards where *Upholder* might be expected. Woodward arrived at the aftermath of the attack in the early dawning, delighted to find that Wanklyn had left him such a sitter. He sensed there had been trouble. He had no definite idea where Wanklyn was now—not that he minded much at this particular moment, for he saw this fat target lit by the faint flush from the east and stopped still, with two destroyers near by, not noticeably interested much in anything.

Woodward manœuvred into a perfect position up-sun and was only a matter of seconds from firing at *Oceania*, when he saw two columns of water gush up from the other side of the ship—and heard two obvious torpedo explosions rattle *Unbeaten*. He could still hardly believe it as the water which spurted and shot over the fated ship was spraying out and settling again.

"Well, I'll be——!"

It must have been more than galling to have sighted the convoy the previous day, been unable to attack it, and now to have exercised such initiative in moving over, only to find a helpless victim and then at the very last gasp to have it snatched from his sight.

Woodward watched *Oceania* sink through his periscope, and so saved his torpedoes.

In his usual way Wanklyn worried a lot about the consequences of his attack, and tossed—a tired man—as he lay for an hour or two later that day in his bunk off duty. Crawford confirmed afterwards how he felt. Wanklyn could never quite reconcile the needs of war with his own real nature—nor could he always justify his actions to himself. But it was war. And they were all in it now. He had to think of his crew. And transports sunk meant the Eighth Army's victory quicker, and less Britons lost. Things got so complicated once one started to compare the pro's and con's. So he just snatched some sleep instead. When he woke he felt better. Perhaps it was that he had been very tired. He did not know.

Meanwhile, what about *Ursula* and *Upright* all this

time? The action was not over yet. Both received the signals from *Unbeaten* and *Upholder*. Hezlet, in *Ursula*, had plenty of time to adjust his position to meet the course of events. But Wraith was not so lucky. He was well to the north of the enemy's track and promptly sped south.

If the *Vulcania* and her escort had not swept from the scene of disaster so quickly, Wraith would have been in time for a shot at something. But, as it was, he found himself dead ahead of the destroyer—so had to dive. This put a premature end to his chances of attacking a ship doing some twenty-three knots—three times the submarine's speed.

But *Ursula* still stood ready to try and put down the surviving ship. Hezlet sighted an M.A.S. coming from the direction of Tripoli, which passed fairly close, and he felt sure that it would be going out to meet the convoy, and that he was consequently in roughly the right position.

He kept a keen look-out into the glare of the sun, and spotted a large ship and one destroyer steaming at speed.

"Damn," he muttered, "they're farther south than I expected. We can't get near enough for a sure success."

Nevertheless, he closed as far as he could and let fire a salvo. He aimed at bow, amidships, and stern for complete coverage, but could hardly expect a hit at that range.

"Down periscope."

Hezlet could not wait to see if he had got on the mark, but heard an explosion about the time expected. As soon as it was wise he took *Ursula* up again and saw, to his delight, that the ship had a starboard list, which made

Vulcania look as if she were going to sleep sitting up. Hezlet plotted her course over a considerable period and calculated that her speed had reduced quite a bit—although he still could not catch her.

"At least we've winged her," Hezlet told his Number One, "so back to Malta—can't do anything else here."

There were congratulations and jubilation all round for the submariners when they reached the sanctuary of Lazaretto—for such it still seemed to them. Two ships sunk and one damaged out of a convoy of three. A brave blow, which would have a more far-reaching effect than its immediate set-back to the enemy—for it would make them pause and ponder how long they dare to send troops to Africa at all if the chances of arrival were to be so slim.

Some speculation and mystery surrounded Hezlet's attack on the *Vulcania*. By this time Wellington bombers were visiting Tripoli on many nights from Malta, so the obvious thing would be for the ship to be turned round at the port in the shortest space of time. Reconnaissance revealed that she had reached Tripoli, and that she had possibly sustained some damage.

If she were able to get to Tripoli, however, she would presumably be able to leave again and return to Italy for any necessary repairs. As she seemed definitely damaged, it looked unlikely that she would take the longer and more dangerous route to Taranto or Messina. Far more likely she would coast-crawl close to Tunisia at the best speed she could muster and then make a dash aiming for Palermo or Naples.

Utmost was patrolling off the north-west corner of Sicily, so Cayley was warned accordingly. "Expect to see *Vulcania*. Try to intercept and sink."

K

"We've got Cayley in the right area, Geoffrey," said Simpson; "now let's lay on air reconnaissance to give him all the gen. possible."

"Very good, sir—leave it to me."

No time was wasted in this Malta war. Next day aircraft reported *Vulcania* north-bound to the west of the island. She had wasted no time, either, and was well on her way. And, to the plane crew's utter astonishment, she was cracking along at her full speed of twenty-three knots.

"Seems fantastic," grumbled Tanner in the Operations Room. "She shouldn't be able to manage more than about fifteen knots. Damned queer."

Anyway, Cayley was given her present position and course, and he did his best to head her off. But it was no good. Cayley knew he would be within five miles or so of her as she approached. And he was. But the *Vulcania* bustled past *Utmost* on the horizon well out of range.

"Twenty-three knots be blowed—she was doing nearer thirty, I reckon!" he told Ops. after returning. He might have stood a chance if she had been reduced to fifteen knots, but rattling along, a speck on the horizon, at a speed thrice the sub.'s best effort just left Cayley standing and fuming.

There the mystery of the damaged ship stood. Nothing could shake Hezlet's conviction that he had seen the effect of his hit on her. Gradually the episode faded from the minds of the flotilla as fresh operations came along.

Then the Italian soldier's diary made its way to Malta *via* Intelligence, and the mystery was solved.

"We'll have to be more careful about claims in future," the Captain said; "not that anyone can be blamed for the *Vulcania*—it was just one of those odd things that happen."

What in fact did happen was that the sudden disaster to the two other ships in the convoy had keyed every one aboard *Vulcania* and her escorting destroyer to a state of supreme vigilance.

Unobserved by Hezlet, two German aircraft accompanied the enemy ships. And as *Ursula* fired one of these reccy planes spotted the torpedo tracks. *Ursula's* periscope went down, so she saw nothing of this. The aircraft swooped down and dive-bombed the torpedoes, trying to stop them reaching the ship.

The look-outs on *Vulcania* saw the diving plane and cried out:

"Torpedoes starboard."

All the troops on deck rushed over to one side. The captain ordered full starboard helm, to turn the ship stern on to the tracks. The torpedoes were exploded by the plane short of the ship, accounting for the bang heard in the sub. The sudden rush of the troops across the deck and the effect of helm explained the list Hezlet saw when he came up to periscope depth. And this sudden change of course while travelling fast solved the report of reduced speed.

So the story was complete. The first report had reached Malta at 0531 on the day of that before-dawn attack, saying that one transport had been sunk. Now the last details were discovered, months afterwards. So only two out of three could be claimed. But it was still an example of perfect team-work, from planning the trap and the R.A.F.'s reconnaissance, to the magnificent manœuvres of David Wanklyn as he overcame all obstacles to record his proudest patrol.

"Actually," Tubby Crawford told Tanner at Lazaretto over a cup of coffee—the beer had run out till the next supplies got through—"I think the *Oceania* op. was Wanklyn's best to date. More brilliant than the V.C. job—though that was terrific, too."

14

A HIT—BY ACCIDENT

LIEUTENANT-COMMANDER CAYLEY made up for his abortive patrol waiting for the *Vulcania* quite soon afterwards. On a dark autumn night he sighted three Italian cruisers steaming at twenty knots and escorted by several destroyers.

He fired at a range of a little less than a mile: a nice distance for aiming and just far enough away to elude any counter-attack. The torpedoes ran their course. Then a fantastic flash as a cruiser was hit just abaft the foremost funnel. A mushroom-shaped crimson flare shot up more than two hundred feet and stayed there—suspended—for several seconds. Night became day. *Utmost* lay on the surface, naked, unashamed—and unhappy. Cayley closed the hatch in a hurry, leapt the last rung of the ladder down to the control-room—and took her down in a desperate dive.

The cruiser sank. *Utmost* escaped.

Wanklyn went on. Patrol the seventeenth. An attack made by moonlight only an hour after leaving Lazaretto. Result: a Perla-class U-boat sunk. She must have been waiting for a chance to pounce on shipping sailing to or from Malta. Instead—she was sunk by a single torpedo.

Then on the same patrol Wanklyn got a signal saying that a force of British cruisers and destroyers—*Aurora, Penelope, Lance,* and *Lively*—was leaving Malta to intercept an important enemy convoy that had been sighted heading eastward from Messina. Just on midnight *Upholder* spotted the British ships at speed astern and approaching the sub. Wanklyn dived to "let them through." He heard their racing propellers and smiled. So different from the agony of anticipation when enemy engines throbbed through the water above the little sub. An hour later they opened fire. *Upholder* watched the fight from a position eight miles north-westward. Forty-eight minutes passed, and our surface ships had smashed the enemy convoy.

0225. Wanklyn spoke to some of the force as it passed on the way back to Malta, then he set course for the blazing remains to see if there were any pickings. He reached the scene by 0400. Three darkened ships were manœuvring near by; but, as two of them looked like single-funnel destroyers identical to *Lance* and *Lively*, he dare not risk an attack before daylight in case of any mistakes.

First light.

"They're not ours, after all," Wanklyn announced, as he lowered the periscope. He fired once—and hit one of the destroyers, which were lying stopped. The sub. then withdrew to watch developments. A captain could not afford to make a single error or fail to take the fullest precautions.

Wanklyn had three torpedoes left now, and hoped for still bigger game. The air was alive with the drone of enemy reconnaissance planes. He kept at periscope depth and saw the damaged destroyer taken in tow by another. He had to keep out of range of their listening gear all the time. He stalked them from the northward, and, as no better targets looked likely to come into his periscope picture, he decided to attack the undamaged destroyer.

At that instant two cruisers came over the horizon. They approached at speed, in line ahead and zigzagging, with a destroyer of the Aviere class on either beam.

"Change of plan," Wanklyn said shortly.

He manœuvred *Upholder* into an attacking position. The first cruiser was too quick, but the other one would be a possible. He fired his last three torpedoes at the rear cruiser.

The first torpedo ran ahead of the target—and blew the bows off the destroyer on the far wing! "That's what you call a fluke," he said.

The second torpedo sped steadily towards the target. "Keep your fingers crossed, Tubby." It got a ship's length from the cruiser. Then came a shock: the gyro failed, and it wandered crazily off its course. So near a success.

The third also ran ahead of the cruiser on the far wing, hit the same unfortunate destroyer for a second time—and sank it! Perhaps it was luck, perhaps not. Wanklyn might have made sure that they overlapped before firing. He did not admit it, but then he was always modest. It had been a hectic thirty-six hours.

"Quite like a short week-end," some one in the mess said.

"What's that? Never heard of it. Not for years and years anyway."

On to the twentieth patrol. *Upholder* was destined to be dogged by a series of setbacks. She attacked and damaged a tanker, but one torpedo, instead of running in the direction and plane aimed, spun in a spiral to the bottom beneath *Upholder*. It exploded with a shattering crack, and shook the sub. severely.

"Never a dull moment," came the inevitable comment from the mess!

Upholder surfaced and attacked with gunfire, but accurate aim from two Breda guns forced Wanklyn to dive. He could not afford to risk a hit on the casing or conning-tower while she was surfaced—or *Upholder* could sink in a few seconds.

On the same patrol when on his way back to base Wanklyn met the U-boat *St Bon*. The enemy saw *Upholder* first, though, and also had the advantage of the light. This was to be a battle, with Wanklyn at a disadvantage. *Upholder* dived. He fired one tube unavailingly as he did so.

Then he made a series of startlingly spectacular turns, until he decided he had brought the boat into a good position. He rose to periscope depth and sent his last torpedo speeding straight for the enemy. *St Bon* sank.

So, on again to the twenty-first, -second, and -third patrols, during which they sank another U-boat, two more supply ships, and a trawler. On an 'Ægean Cruise' a caïque carrying some German technicians fell a victim to *Upholder*. The same day another caïque and a small schooner were added to the toll. Next night they caught yet another caïque, and then while surfaced spotted an auxiliary schooner and a trio of caïques, crammed with Germans. One caïque and the schooner went down; a second caïque escaped; *Upholder* drew alongside the third.

One of the Nazis started to pull the pin out of a hand-grenade to toss it on *Upholder*. Some one shot him dead. A second German drew his revolver. But he got a bullet through the brain and splashed into the night waters among the Greek islands. Moonlight shone on the spray for a second. Wanklyn destroyed the caïque, battened down the conning-tower, and dived—with one torpedo left. Just after breakfast an Italian tanker sailed past. It was now or never. He got his sights on her—and made no mistake.

By the end of 1941 Wanklyn was nearing the completion of his round of duty, and Simpson asked him if he would like to return to the United Kingdom. But Wanklyn replied characteristically:

"Thanks, sir—but no. It's my ambition to sail back home in command of *Upholder*."

He had one-eighth of a million tons of merchant shipping to his credit. Twenty-two chevrons appeared on his Jolly Roger, one for each ship sunk.

Yes, it had been a long, long time since *Upholder* sailed out of *Dolphin* that dawn of a year and more ago. Fort Blockhouse. He could barely bring it to mind for a moment. Then he remembered the day. Gosport Hard . . . Camber and Nicholson's yacht-yard . . . the thin line of Portsdown Hill in the distance . . . the first ferry-boat in the harbour . . . *Upholder* slipping out to Spithead . . . past the grey walls at the entrance to Portsmouth Harbour . . . beyond Haslar, last link with the shore. He dearly wanted to bring *Upholder* home again when her term was through. Meanwhile he must stay with her.

He thought of Betty. Of the brief years they had been

together. Barely two years out of a lifetime. But Wanklyn's life could not be measured in months or years. Into
his thirty-one years he had crowded half a dozen lives'
excitement, achievement, and honour. As one commander put it: "He had judgment and ability far beyond
his years." And he managed to communicate it to all
his crew.

A bar to the D.S.O. came with the sinking of the
U-boat *St Bon*. A second bar was added for the work on
his twenty-third patrol. But how much longer . . .?

15

FRIDAY THE THIRTEENTH

THE long, languid Mediterranean summer came and went. And all the while the 10th Submarine Flotilla came and went too. Through the autumn, till the onset of winter, the only hazards the submarines faced were operational. And they were hazards enough, without what was soon to follow. Stopping as suddenly as it had started, the Luftwaffe carried out its last sortie against Malta from 1940–41 winter quarters in Sicily on May 11, 1941. Then they went eastward to put into practice all they had learnt over the island. Malta had been a rehearsal for Russia. Even though they were not yet even at war with the Soviet states.

So for seven months, from May to December 1941, Malta became once more a comparatively pleasant place to be in: an island of sun, subs., and the smell of oil—or so it seemed to the staff at Lazaretto. The respite from raids gave the island its chance to finish off adequate amenities and shelters.

By the time December came, the preparation was fairly complete. The only other aerial activities during these summer and autumn months since the Luftwaffe left were the regular but restricted night visits of

Mussolini's rather erratic and eccentric Regia Aero-nautica.

But every one knew in their hearts that this spell free from the Germans could not last for ever. As inevitably as the seasons, with winter came the Luftwaffe again. In earnest, this time—not just rehearsing.

At Lazaretto Simpson saw that the best possible pre-parations were made. For it was no use relying on the fortunate fact that during the previous winter's four-month visitation no serious damage had been done to the submarines or the sub. base itself. Nor that both targets had escaped being singled out for attack.

Simpson remembered the fury and ferocity even in that winter, culminating in the combined mining and bombing raids during the nights of March and April. They had resulted in innumerable loads landing on Manoel Island and in the harbour. True, the net result as far as H.M.S. *Talbot* was concerned amounted to one piglet killed. But the flotilla could not count on being blessed with luck always.

In those days, of course, there had been no shelters to speak of; they were still in the course of construction by the resident miners, whose habit was to stop work dur-ing all air-raid alarms. So the shelters progressed slowly through that spring of 1941.

The people of Malta showed a pathetic faith in the safety of the Lazaretto shelters. They would have their sleeping-quarters above ground and trek down to the vault-roof store-rooms below. These shelters consisted firstly of a tunnel hewn out of the rock a few feet behind the ends of the store-rooms. Each of the store-rooms had an entrance to this tunnel, which ran the whole length of the inhabited buildings. When the tunnel was completed further tunnelling into the rock was undertaken to form offices and dormitories.

A short tunnel ran straight into the rock from the first courtyard. It was actually an old excavation with a light railway track running along it. About a hundred feet from the entrance a vertical shaft shot up into the open air. Dark, dank, and noisy it all was; but fitted with a double tier of canvas bunks and electric light—when it could be installed later—this served as an additional shelter and had the advantage of an exit at each end. Something that might mean the difference between living and dying. So by December adequate shelter had been created for every one during the daytime, and sleeping space for about half the Lazaretto personnel at night.

After some 200 days the loathed Luftwaffe reappeared over Malta, on December 5. Their long and unlamented absence was at an end.

They came at first only on reconnaissance to spy out the lie of the island since their last sorties. A fortnight later to the day, on December 19, their operations started seriously. The Germans spurned any Italian aid during daylight, and left the little Regia Aeronautica to carry on in the more comforting and safer hours of darkness.

At first it began to look as if once again the submarines would not be considered worth attention. All the attacks were aimed against airfields and the dockyard. The Germans' policy paid, too, for it began to become apparent that they could get bolder and bolder. They were relentlessly wresting the initiative from the Royal Air Force.

Always inadequate, the R.A.F.'s fighter strength was

slowly but surely whittled away. Seen from the present safety of Lazaretto, it seemed miraculous how any aircraft at all could be operating from airfields which were receiving systematic, pitiless pounding day after day.

That side of the story is already history: how Malta magnificently survived the bludgeoning of bombs without surrender to become Malta, G.C. Over at Lazaretto the submariners would watch the daily doses.

A sailor ashore from sub. patrol cocked an eye over to Valletta and expressed his simple sympathy.

"The poor b——s aren't 'arf copping it."

This view was far more frequently found than the opposite one, the classic "Damn you, Jack—I'm inboard." The latter outlook might be understandable sometimes, but the matelots realized—like every one else on the island—that they were all in it together. The water lapping round the shore stressed this. There was no going back, no escape. This was it. Malta lived or died. And so did they.

They would hardly have been human, though, if they had not thanked their stars that so far Lazaretto remained more or less unscathed.

So the first few days, before and after Christmas, were watched by the men of *Talbot* almost as outsiders. Yet they felt an affinity to the fighter aircraft who were struggling for survival.

The results of one raid were that only *two* Hurricanes could claw their way into the air when the next wave of forty Junkers throbbed across the coast for another attack. Over at Lazaretto, they watched in silence as these two lone fighters took on overwhelming, unbelievable odds. And then, another time, when the vein-straining efforts of the ground staff managed to get nine Hurricanes climbing to combat, a feeling of thankfulness swept over the spectators to this one-sided battle above their heads.

Then the odds became longer. The enemy sent over a fighter for every five bombers. If the meagre Hurricanes went for the bombers the Messerschmitts jumped them back before they could get in. If they concentrated on the Me's, the bombers got away with it. And it was the bombers that did the damage. So the Hurricanes forsook the fighters to try to bring down the bombers before they reached their objectives. The results which they notched in terms of Junkers shot up were out of all proportion to the few fighters the R.A.F. had. They qualified again and again to rank with the Famous Few of 1940.

The gathering around the loud-speaker in the Lazaretto mess listened to the level tones of Alvar Liddell on the nine o'clock news from London stating:

"During daylight to-day two hundred Spitfires carried out a sweep over Northern France without meeting any opposition."

Tanner looked livid. "How hopelessly unfair it seems. Two hundred planes and no opposition. Those poor pilots over at the airfield know where there's some opposition, all right. What wouldn't they give for a handful of those Spitfires! A dozen would do for a start. No opposition—huh!"

There were murmurs of agreement all round. The mess seemed quiet that night.

What was still more galling was that while our ground staffs did the impossible to keep the few fighters flying, over in Sicily, only seventy miles away, Kesselring's ground crews were working absolutely undisturbed all day—with a full night's rest thrown in, too. So it went on. Airfields, dockyard, airfields, dockyard—they were all attacked.

On December 28, R.T. Interceptions informed Submarine Headquarters that a small force of Messerschmitts had just been told to attack two submarines about to enter harbour. This was a brilliant piece of radio work. *Urge* and *Upholder* had been spotted by reconnaissance planes heading for harbour after exercising with *Beryl*. A couple of the Me's shot out of the sun as the subs. were surfaced.

Woodward was up top on *Urge*.

"Crash dive," he ordered. The sub. was below in a matter of seconds. Woodward heard the splutter of machine-gun fire on the water lapping over the hatch. He had shut it just in time.

Norman, temporarily commanding *Upholder*, was not so lucky. He saw the planes streaking down on him. Before he could say a word *Upholder* was hit by five cannon and a mass of machine-gun bullets. They peppered spray all round the sub.

"Dive," Pat Norman shouted.

But a cannon shell burst inside the bridge at the second he said it. He staggered to a rail for support, with multiple wounds. He groped to the conning-tower hatch as the second plane came in. Somehow he got through it and shut it behind him. By then *Upholder* was diving.

"Are you all right?" Number One asked anxiously.

"Yes. But take over, will you?"

Norman was severely wounded, but the sub. slunk back to base safely and he recovered. *Upholder* sailed according to schedule two days later, with Wanklyn in command.

This practice of beating up submarines entering or leaving harbour rapidly became much too common—so menacing, in fact, that subs. returning from patrol had orders to remain submerged the whole way up the searched channel, right up to the harbour entrance itself. Then if no red flag were seen through the periscope flying from the Palace tower as a warning of a raid in progress they could surface just outside the boom defences and enter harbour. If the flag were flying they had to hang around until it came down. After all the perils of a patrol this was very irritating. The crews hated the new procedure, but it had to be done for safety. Simpson just could not risk losing submarines on his own doorstep.

And on the first night of the year 1942 the Germans tried out a new weapon. They dropped a small number of rocket bombs from a height of 5000 feet or so. These bombs were intended to give greater accuracy and penetrating power—and also to strike terror into the inhabitants of the island. As it transpired, no bomb fell within the harbour area. Moreover, their noise, though terrific, did not terrify. The luminous trail left by the bombs attracted attention and gave people an immediate consolation when it was obvious that the missile would, in fact, fall clear of them. This type of raid was not repeated; at any rate, no one at Lazaretto ever saw them again.

"Quite like a free fireworks show," some one on the veranda at Lazaretto called, beckoning the few folk still in the mess to come out and see it. So the rocket bombs were received philosophically by the population.

L

Raids, raids, raids. On January 6 a single aircraft slipped in unobserved and dropped a stick of bombs through low winter cloud. They fell right across No. 1 berth in the dockyard. One of these caused twenty-six perforations in the pressure-hull of H.M. Submarine P31, which was in dock for her periodical maintenance check. Three minor casualties occurred and damage to the steering gear delayed the sub.'s sailing by three weeks. Instead of leaving on the 8th, she set out on her next patrol on January 29.

P33 and P32 were sunk. And now P31 was damaged. Nowhere was safe. Before P31's steering gear had been repaired *Unbeaten* was attacked by a group of Messerschmitt 109's. The sub. was returning from patrol, and proceeded on the surface only two miles from the harbour entrance. She survived the assault, but it was this pointer to what might be expected that led to Simpson's orders for entry into Malta. Subs. were to surface one mile from St Elmo lighthouse, and then only provided that the red flag was not flying from the Castille. The commanding officer was not to come to the bridge before the sub. was within the breakwater.

Subsequently, on two separate occasions *Sokol* was surprised by fighters only five hundred yards from the harbour entrance, when she was just going over to Grand Harbour and not out on patrol at all. As the purpose of her trip each time was battery repairs, she could not dive but managed to ward them off with gunfire. It was going to take more than a Messerschmitt to sink *Sokol*, Commander Karnicki told himself, as the planes veered off in some disorder from the sub.'s accurate gunfire.

On February 8 P38 started a patrol off Kuriat. Later

the Admiralty announced with regret that she was over-
due and must be presumed lost. Six subs. had been lost
in fourteen months: six out of a total of twenty.

Meanwhile the raids intensified, and after eight weeks
of comparative immunity the blow fell on Lazaretto—
perhaps on the very day that P38 went down.

Most sailors dislike a Friday, and nearly all of them
hate the thirteenth day of the month. So when the two
coincide, as on Friday, February 13, the worst can
happen. This day it did.

The dawn broke brightly, but with eight-tenths' low
cloud. Aircraft thundering overhead as usual occasionally came through these clouds to drop a stick of bombs.
The accustomed midday raid found the *Talbot* ratings
at their meal, and most of the officers gathered on the
veranda outside their mess before going in for lunch.

With stark suddenness, aircraft appeared screaming
over the sub. base. A large stick exploded across the
creek, some of the bombs in the creek itself, some on
the Valletta bastions. There was no time to think or
move. A second stick whistled and whined out of the
clouds, and crashed along Pieth Creek. One made a
mess of the house of the General Officer Commanding,
Malta. Another stick, in the headwaters of Lazaretto
Creek, convinced the submariners that this was the
start.

Luckily the pilots were keen to keep up in the clouds
as much as possible, to escape any lone Hurricane that
might be about and to blind the anti-aircraft gunners.
The bombers' aim was erratic, and Lazaretto was still
unscarred. But they had not long to wait for the second
shot.

The first raid was half an hour after noon. The second started at 2.30. But before it began Captain Simpson ordered that at the next alarm every one was to go to ground. The long-awaited attempt on Lazaretto had come at last—and he was running no risks that could be avoided. He had a flotilla of submarines to service and protect—and several hundred men too.

The officers had lunch. The weather cleared. By 1430, when the sirens sounded for the fourth time that day, the sky was without a cloud. Most personnel took cover carefully as soon as the warning went. For they could only count on a few seconds while the enemy came in from the sea. The staff officer, Geoffrey Tanner, and the doctor sat in the heavily sand-bagged mine-watching post. Periscope patrols were forgotten for the moment.

"Looks like the airfields are for it again," Tanner said. "Poor old Luqa. Still, sooner them than us!"

They were watching five Junkers 88's, with fighters weaving above them, coming in from the north. Spinola and Fort Manoel blazed away with ack-ack.

Hardly were Tanner's rather uncharitable words out of his mouth when the planes banked steeply over Gzira and made a shallow dive straight for Lazaretto. The sudden turn threw the A.A. gunners off aim for a moment. Tanner and the doctor saw the Ju's coming in to the creek with shell-bursts well behind them. The gunners quickly corrected their aim, and the bombers dived down through a cloud of bursts.

"Crippen! They've got him," yelled the staff officer, as something snapped off and fluttered from the starboard wing of the leading aircraft. But, hit or not, the plane kept its course and the two men saw a couple of remarkable 'things' leave the belly of the aircraft. They were no normal bombs. They looked like outsize dustbins slowly tumbling over and over towards them. The men became almost mesmerized, and all but failed to see similar objects falling from the other four machines. For long-drawn, nerve-racking seconds they watched the missiles.

"Do you think they'll fall short—or overshoot? Or——" Tanner left the sentence. The two bins might do neither, but decide to descend on the mine-watching post itself.

"Thank God. They're dropping short." They relaxed a little and looked around at the other planes. Then their world shattered into a shambles of noise, blast, dust, and water.

The first two G-mines—not dustbins after all—landed squarely on Lazaretto, flattening the sick-quarters and mess-decks. Others fell in the water, out of sight behind the buildings; one struck the rocky shore opposite; the rest, a salvo, straddled the water just in front of the look-out post.

Tanner and the doctor had been in the right spot—a mine-watching post, watching mines. The mines that dropped near the look-out post nearly caught a party of submariners on leave, who had chosen to take a quiet afternoon's sail in a gig. Mines met the water on each side of the boat. This was the salvation of the scared occupants, as the two blasts must have been equalized —so saving both the boat and crew from disintegration. Tanner saw the gig vanish behind two colossal columns of dirty water, and never expected to see it again. To Tanner's amazement, when the water and the noise subsided there was the boat, rocking wildly but floating quite untouched.

"Where's the crew?" the doctor yelled.

Then they could not suppress a smile as one, then another, and another head bobbed above the gunwale! Until all six of the shaken crew could be seen staring uncomfortably about them as they hung on to the boat for dear life! All of them were ready to duck once more behind the reassuring—but quite useless—shelter of the wooden half-inch of the boat's sides.

The new mines were made of just thin shells full of high explosive. They burst on impact and relied entirely on blast for their effect. The Germans must have realized that they would be good weapons to use against Malta. The island's stone buildings localized the effect of more ordinary bombs, which would be likely to demolish only the house it hit, whereas the big blast from a G-mine was enough to rock the thin walls of the more modern houses so that their roofs and floors fell in. Against the older buildings and battlements the mines' bark was worse than their bite. The casualties in this first attack on Lazaretto amounted to three killed and five wounded. Considering the brutal blast from the mines and the material damage done, these figures were encouragingly low, and due to the warning attack two hours earlier. But every life lost became a blow to the flotilla and Simpson himself—whether happening underwater or at Lazaretto.

A further attack in the afternoon caused no casualties nor damage—but helped the superstitious sailor to confirm his already strong belief that Friday the thirteenth was a bad day in every way.

As a result of these raids, Simpson acted at once, and had the old store-houses in the ground-floor cleared of all their contents. New mess-decks were satisfactorily created within ten days, and decks which led direct to the rock shelters. This afforded increased safety for Lazaretto personnel, as there was now no need to go out of doors at all to get to the rock shelters. Apart from the humanitarian aspect, the measure also had its practical point: for unless the maintenance staff at base were safe and well no submarines could be serviced and in time no patrols run.

The relentless raids on Malta continued daily. But Lazaretto was left out of the Luftwaffe's scheme for a full fortnight. Yet no one believed that they would be satisfied with the results of the 13th. These were comparatively negligible, and did not affect the operation of the flotilla—yet.

On Friday 27, another Friday, it came as no surprise when the enemy returned to the sub. base. Despite the blast of the G-mines, they were apparently dissatisfied with the weapons' comparative inefficiency, so hurled 1000-kilo armour-piercing bombs: 2000 lb., no less.

The officers shifted into their shelters, and the sound outside reached a crescendo far worse than they had ever heard before—and through it all the ceaseless stutter of the four-barrelled machine-gun, manned by Maltese, in a sand-bagged emplacement on the water's edge.

Then loud and clear above all the din came the screech and scream of a Junkers 87 diving, its guns blazing. There were two eruptive explosions. Every one in the shelter was shaken, and all the lights went out. A furore of dust-laden air rushing through the tunnel. Above the rush and roar the sound of the multiple machine-gun could be heard still firing at the plane as it zoomed up and away.

In a few minutes the raid was over. The officers emerged to find that one bomb had burst at the corner of their block, and the other so close to the machine-gun post that the sand-bagged redoubt was perched on the very edge of the crater. Yet the gunners had kept their weapons working the whole time—as the plane came diving down at them, during the actual explosion a few feet off, and afterwards until the enemy flew out of range.

Captain Simpson made a special commendation on the conduct of these island gunners.

Most of the officers' quarters were reduced to rubble, and six of them had not been quick enough in reaching shelter. The rubble buried and killed four of them. The other two were just leaving the veranda by the steps below it when the bombs exploded nearby. Neither remembered much about it after that for several seconds. Then they found themselves flat on their faces, quite unhurt, with roofing stones and huge wooden beams all around them.

Still the submarines operated unaffected by the Luftwaffe; but the base began to find it daily more difficult to 'keep them floating,' although the damage resulted only in discomfort and put nothing vital out of action. The submarine officers on leave were sent to sleep out; base officers remained sleeping in rock shelters; and all of them messed in the ratings' dining-room. The ward-room was reconstructed by the end of March in a store previously full of drain-pipes.

Clothes, gear, and furniture were saved from the wrecked cabins of the officers' quarters and stored in the dank shelters, where they soon grew a fine coating of mould. Most of the submarine officers moved into flats at Sliema and St Julian's Bay, leaving the base officers the cheerless but safe shelters.

Close to Lazaretto, outside the ramparts of Fort Manoel, stood a gigantic tumulus. Beneath it lay buried almost empty fuel-oil tanks, one of the few essentials to have been transferred safely underground well before the War. At one end of this tomb-like mound was a considerable space hewn out of the solid rock. This was converted into a combined dormitory and row of offices. The new abode was approached by a long flight of steep steps. Constantly dripping water made them slippery and slithery, while the walls ran with moisture that struck a shivery chill when going down from the heat outside. The stench from the fuel-oil took some getting used to. But, despite the disadvantages, the Cavern—as it was christened—made a splendid shelter, where work and sleep could be carried on during the heaviest raid. Once they had got used to the racket overhead.

So ended the first two attacks on the submarine base. Preparations had been made and schemes scheduled to enable the flotilla to go on operating if any particular part of Lazaretto should be obliterated. The air war worsened, but so far difficulties were being overcome. But the base was in the balance.

16

HARBOURING DANGER

THE overriding object of the 10th Flotilla remained to patrol the Mediterranean, and search out and sink every enemy ship possible. Four or more raids a day must not blind Simpson to the fact. And all through January and February they carried on this task. On into the last eight weeks, too, they still sank ships. Wanklyn was operating with his customary brilliance, and Simpson asked him to come into his office on March 1.

"David"—Simpson motioned his ace commander into a chair—"you've done twenty-three patrols now."

Wanklyn knew what was coming, and got his word in first.

"Yes, Shrimp—but I'd like to stay on for another couple of months. I can boost the bag a lot more yet."

"I know, David—but I'm afraid I can't authorize it. I know how you feel, but you really do need a rest. I'll give you two more. Then back you go—after twenty-five. You know you should have called it a day long before now. It has been a wonderful show, but it can't go on for ever. That's my best offer. Carry on with this next one, then the twenty-fifth, and then I'm packing you off to Pompey."

"But——"

"Now, David—don't be difficult. Fifteen's the normal number. You know that as well as I do."

So Wanklyn agreed. And it would be impossible to begin to do justice to what the flotilla went through in March and April—at Malta and in the Mediterranean. Tired crews became more and more exhausted. No bombers existed on the island now, and only a handful of Fleet Air Arm Swordfish. The submarines and the Swordfish carried on, the only offensive means Malta possessed. But every one was determined to go on.

The raids continued without respite. Not a day without at least one of the many raids being beamed against Lazaretto. When the dockyard or the airfields became the target the submarine base breathed for a few hours. The dust laid. But it was only a breather. Moreover, the fighter defence was dwindling steadily, and the enemy had the air more and more as it pleased.

Life was like this: divided into periods of work with an ear cocked for the siren and an eye open for the red flag fluttering up to the masthead on the Palace tower as warning of imminent danger to the Valletta district; swift dashes to the nearest shelter, with spells in its catacomb-like atmosphere listening to the uproar outside and wondering what changes would meet the eye on emergence; and a return to work when it was all over. Then it started again. Day and night. The catacombs were getting like the control-room of a sub. No one knew in the end what time it was, whether light or dark outside.

Moving about Malta became a matter of judging the intervals between raids. To make a mistake might mean

being stranded too far from shelter. And that could all
too easily be fatal.

Frequently the island had Air Raid Warning conditions for hours on end, but the actual raids came as
short, sharp jabs—with waves of aircraft awaiting their
turn to come in and have a crack. The Germans proved
as methodical as ever, so it was still generally possible to
judge when it was safe to snatch a wash or a meal or
visit the heads, undisturbed.

One of the most amazing things that happened at
Lazaretto was that, despite all the damage, neither the
galley nor the hot-water system received enough enemy
attention to be put out of action. Hot meals and showers
were therefore always available, although the former
had to be eaten to a background of gaping holes in the
floor and ceiling—and the latter taken without the
privacy of walls in the bathrooms.

After the opening phase, moreover, casualties in the
flotilla were practically nil—an amazing fact; and
damage to submarines was far less than it might have
been. Strange as it seems, it was fatigue and physical
discomfort combined that were finally crippling the
capacity to continue. But the worst eight weeks were
still to come.

Meanwhile the sojourns in the Caverns were lightened
by many amusing incidents and yarns. Tommo was in a
mood for memories as he sat there with Tanner on the
day the intensive raids on Lazaretto started. They
swopped stories of subs. and got around to the First
World War.

"I've just remembered a true tale my father told me,
Geoffrey. Apparently some of our subs. patrolled near
the Dardanelles off Turkey in that war. And one day the

skipper of one sub. came up to periscope depth offshore to take the usual look around. Well, the vision was totally black. But the time was midday, so something was radically wrong."

"Well, what was it?"

"He checked the depth, and also saw that the periscope was working properly. So the only thing he could do was take a peep out of the second periscope. And what do you think he saw? Only a few feet away a swarthy Turkish fisherman was hanging out of his boat and his hand was over the periscope lens trying to yank the whole thing up out of the sea! Some story, eh?"

The unquenchable Tomkinson had never been better, as bombs burst above and reverberated in the giant empty fuel tanks beside the sheltered quarters. Somehow they found fun from it all. They laid bets on how long the electric lights would survive, as they wavered, flickered, eclipsed, and then glowed again: groans first, then the glow greeted by cheers of encouragement; finally, cries of disgust as the lights went out for good.

The gloom would be relieved by the feeble glimmer from a couple of oil-lamps. The staff tried desperately to work normally by placing their papers as near the lamps as they dared; and between raids Captain Simpson, with his secretary and Chief Writer, would sit at little tables in the sun-drenched courtyard outside the shelter entrance. As soon as the sirens sounded again the typewriter would be ceremoniously carried back to safety. They mingled with a mælstrom of people hurrying up from the base. Then, with his tin hat perched on his head, Simpson would clamber up and survey the scene from the top of the mound covering the Cavern. When he finally thought the raid was really on he would descend into the depths.

Latecomers of lesser rank than his own were always assured of a withering welcome—especially as they were usually heralded by a burst of activity above. They came scampering down the steps at a brisk pace—that interminable flight that gave an immediate impression of descending into Hades.

Once a small bomb went off close to the entrance, and the blast blew a yelling Maltese down the steps right into Tomkinson's lap as the submariner sat cogitating on a camp-bed about how much more useful he would have been at sea in *Urge*.

"Come right in!" said Tommo. "Plenty of room inside, if it's full on top!"

After prolonged periods of quiet Tanner would phone to find out if they could safely ascend into the sun and air again. They staggered up the steps countless times, and blinked at a huge cloud of brown dust and smoke that hung over the last target. A streak of silver and a white-wisp vapour trail thousands of feet up indicated a marauding Messerschmitt. It was useless to waste ammunition on a fighter flying at that height, until it swooped low enough to get a staccato spurt of machine-gun fire. And once more Malta could relapse into the warm, welcome peace of a spring day to tend its wounds and await the next round. She couldn't hit back. She wouldn't throw in the towel.

The day after Simpson saw Wanklyn about his return home came the first damage to submarines. During a heavy attack on the Lazaretto on March 2, bombs exploding in the creeks sent splinters shattering through parts like periscopes, and the shock-waves cracked battery cells. *Upright* was on the verge of leaving for the United Kingdom after many active patrols, when she suffered battery damage in this way. It was ironic that the day before she was due to sail she should get hit. It was a couple of weeks before her repairs could be completed. Eventually she sailed on the 19th with only one battery section.

In the evening of the 2nd *Talbot* suffered a severe personal blow. Tanner was watching another raid a little way off when he suddenly saw a house on the hill hit. It was where the Senior Medical Officer of H.M.S. *Talbot* had been staying, but Tanner did not know whether he or anyone was in it at the time. Tragically, he was. Surgeon Captain Cheeseman did not live to see the last weeks' stand of the subs. at Lazaretto.

Three days later there was a series of attacks on Manoel Island, but no damage was done to subs. or establishments, although all electric lights and telephones were put out of action for the third time. The next day dive-bombers roared down from the south-east sky and very nearly bombed *Una* and P36. Half an hour later a second wave of bombers struck the fuelling lighter moored forty feet from P39. The lighter at once caught fire and sank—dowsing the whole place in shale-oil. More serious, the submarine sustained extensive damage: 172 cell-containers were cracked, warheads knocked off torpedoes, bed-plates of auxiliary machinery smashed, and many welded brackets inside the submarine snapped. She had to be towed to the dockyard for repairs. *Una* and P36 too became temporary casualties; P36 had to be patched in two places where the shrapnel penetrated, and her bifocal periscope needed changing due to a splinter perforation.

Simpson had to take drastic action now for the flotilla to carry on, as every submarine in sight from the air became a day-long danger.

At this stage, and in retrospect, it might seem that steps should have been taken to try to forestall attacks on vessels by seeing that the submarines stayed dived during daylight. But in the fourteen months from January 1941 to the beginning of March 1942 over a thousand air-raids had been directed at Malta with negligible damage to subs. As long as that fortunate fact continued Simpson was entirely justified in avoiding the drastic disorganization which would result from sending the subs. to the bottom of the harbour. For a submarine returning from patrol needed dozens of details to be attended to, as well as a spring-clean after each trip. But most important of all was consideration for the crews. That they should spend even part of their time when home in harbour boxed up in their submarines had to be avoided, whatever else Simpson settled: for under the air-raid conditions likely from now on the crews suffered mental strain equal to—or even worse than— when they were on patrol. They might manage for a trip or two in this way, but Simpson rightly remembered that fresh air and sunshine are the lifeblood of a sub-mariner, who cannot operate efficiently without them. Even ashore, the peace possible for them was little enough now that the siege had started.

Simpson did the best he could. If he had been blessed with two complete crews for each sub. all would have been easier; but, as things were, 90 per cent. of the work which had to be done aboard when in harbour necessarily fell on her own crew—and if the sub. were to stay down all day the work could only be done at night while she was surfaced.

From March 6 the Captain brought the new routine into force—reluctantly. Submarines dived throughout daylight hours at deep-water berths in the harbour, except for one which would occupy the billet actually alongside *Talbot*. The entire repair staff concentrated on this one sub.'s refitting, and then the moment she was finished another one would take her place and the refitted vessel return to the deep-water berth vacated. Any submarines in the dockyard also had to stay on the surface, but as a very necessary precaution they were evacuated of all crew except one officer, an engine-room artificer, and a seaman, who remained in the control-room as an emergency fire-party. If the submarine had no battery on board, however, her entire crew retired to the rock shelter, including the fire-party.

To give crews some sort of rest, Simpson accepted that subs. diving by day could not be fully manned. Half the crew, therefore, went ashore immediately on return from patrol, while the other half had to stay on and man the sub.—to rest as well as they could in the vessel as she lay on the bottom of the harbour while bombs fell far and near at odd times throughout the day. At night-fall they surfaced the sub. to do the necessary work on her during the dark. Then they were ready to dive at dawn—down into their own harbour.

"Might as well be out on patrol," a torpedo-man rightly remarked; "we're down all day and up all night —*and* we have to work at night, too!"

At half-time, when the rest of the crew had spent their week or so of 'relaxation,' the two watches changed

M

places, and the second half-crew prepared the sub. for sea. By this time the 'first watch aboard' had become pretty fed up. Meanwhile, the second crew embarked torpedoes, stores, ammunition, fuel, and food—all at night.

Whichever watch the crew were in, they had the duration of the patrol extended by a week. But perhaps it was the men in the first watch aboard who felt most frustrated. It was worse to add a week on the harbour bottom to the end of a patrol than to come back to the sub. a week early. But no one was pleased. In fact, of course, their berth on the bottom was safer than most spots ashore in March and April.

Commanding officers received the maximum leave and freedom from responsibility, so the first lieutenant or third officer assumed control. Because of this, Simpson frequently found that a third officer of less than a year's experience in a submarine had to take her to a buoy and dive her with half a crew.

"We'd better see that the subs. secure their berthing buoy by the bows only," Simpson told Tanner, "or we may get wires winding round the propellers. It wouldn't be their fault. They're new to it all, and they'll be working in the dark while diving and surfacing."

If a wire did become foul of a propeller it might be many days before the sub. could be used, as divers did not work during air-raids and the island was now rarely free from them. All the while the sub. would be a sitting target.

Forty-eight hours after the routine started P35 dived at dawn, secured to a buoy in seventy feet of water near the middle of the harbour. She had a slight headway on as she submerged, and the pressure-hull under the

T.O.T. tank—quite unprotected by the keel—settled on the clump block of the buoy. A hole about six inches square appeared in a flash through the pressure-hull. The tube compartment flooded. The watertight doors were shut. The third officer surfaced the sub. at 0940, but without enough forward buoyancy. She took an alarming angle by the bow—and vanished. A smoke-candle was fired from her ten minutes later.

It was full daylight, and an air-raid started. A diver went down during the raid. He probed about all round the sub. The hatches were securely shut. The working bridge telegraph got a reply from below. During the forenoon the submarine sent messages to the surface through the underwater gun; they were contained in thermometer tubes and a bottle. But they all went astray in the choppy surface of the sea. A diving-boat took up a permanent position over the sub. Then at 1220 she surfaced and was moved to shallow water. It was a nasty morning for the crew and the shore staff. P35 docked on March 11, and her defects took ten days to put right.

In the midst of all this Lieutenant Peter Harrison was commanding P34 in the Mediterranean. On March 14 she attacked and sank the Italian U-boat *Ammiraglio Milo* near Cape Stilo.

"Better pick up survivors," Harrison said.

He took P34 in and could not help feeling a tinge of pity as he looked down from the bridge to see the Italian crew struggling in the water, splashing near the sub. Fourteen of them were just being brought aboard when a staccato stream of bullets spat across the water from the shore. An Italian shore battery was trying to stop them rescuing the men, but they shoved the enemy crew below quickly and crash-dived—to safety.

Before P35 was ready for service again *Sokol's* momentous month started—March 17 to April 17. *Sokol's* story is interwoven with the whole flotilla during these decisive days. Hers was a story of success in the very worst conditions.

17

"SOKOL'S" MOMENTOUS MONTH

O.R.P. *Sokol* returned from patrol on March 17, and moved straight away into the berth alongside Lazaretto. All the repair staff got to work to fit her for service again and out of this unenviable surface billet. For a month her company struggled for the sub.'s survival. She was chivvied, chased, bombed, blasted, until her epic ended on April 17.

March 17: That first afternoon in the *Talbot* berth the Luftwaffe went on with their all-day bombardment of the sub. base and the warships lying in Grand Harbour.

About 1600 hours a stick of five heavy bombs lined the water between ten and thirty yards from *Sokol*. They burst—and blasted the boat in a succession of sharp explosions. Forty-six battery cells cracked, and *Sokol's* air and water lines were damaged. The telemotor system received a fracture, and every manometer and gauge in the sub. was smashed. Torpedo warheads jumped forward an inch or more. This was just the first day.

March 18: The crew and other hands unloaded her torpedoes under continuous air attack from dawn to dusk. They also tested her batteries. The result of the general examination was never really in doubt: she would have to go around to the dockyard in the Grand Harbour for further repairs—and be exposed day and night as long as the work would take.

March 19: At 1700 *Sokol* started out from Lazaretto to Grand Harbour, but this was not early enough to escape the Luftwaffe. Two Messerschmitt 109's spotted her movement in the still, long-shadowed water, and hurled cannon and machine-gun fire on the luckless *Sokol*. The cannons recorded eight hits on her, but only slight damage was done and no one injured. They put on all possible speed—not very high in her state—and reached the dockyard during the morning—fortunately, to find that almost all the facilities available were those very ones essential to keep the subs. going: the battery shed, where submarine batteries were stored, maintained, and repaired, and the only operable crane with which to hoist the heavy cells in and out of the sub.

But replacing a damaged battery is slow even in the most favourable circumstances: it is a process that just cannot be hurried beyond a certain limit. With the prospect of workmen having to shelter during daytime alerts and operating at night with only a little light and even less gear, the job can be extended almost indefinitely. And all the while *Sokol* lay on the surface.

March 20: The aim was to start changing the damaged cells to-day. But, because of continued heavy air attacks and considerable casualties in the dockyard, the workers quite reasonably refused to be on duty during raids in future. So *Sokol's* cells stayed unchanged. Commander Karnicki paced about the battery shed in one alert and finally decided that the situation was intolerable. He had to order his crew to continue the repair work themselves.

March 21: Work on No. 2 battery was done, miraculously. Also waiting for the dockyard to remedy their defects were *Urge*, P31, and P35. Every effort was made to patch up the submarines especially quickly on the 21st and 22nd, as a convoy's arrival was anticipated the following day, which would bring renewed raids on a heavier scale still. These three subs. were withdrawn from Grand Harbour.

March 22: Other work went on, and *Sokol* was able to leave this very vulnerable spot after dark. To-morrow the convoy was due.

March 23: The convoy came in, as expected. Bedraggled camouflaged ships spread out in Grand Harbour, needing peace but never finding it. The raids came too, even heavier than was feared. *Sokol* and P39 were now alongside the Machinery and Store Wharves respectively.

March 24: Extremely heavy raids against the Grand Harbour and submarine base.

March 25: Lazaretto's turn again. The sub. base bombed heavily.

March 26: Late afternoon now. The dockyard clock had long since stopped. Commander Karnicki's watch showed 1800 hours. The Polish sub. was still by Machinery Wharf on the opposite side of the narrow creek from P39. Sunset.

Then waves of seventy bombers boomed over Grand Harbour in an aggressive assault on the convoy. Every ship was hit. S.S. *Talbot* caught fire and was in dire danger of blowing up: she carried a cargo of ammunition, torpedoes, and big bombs. They had not been able to unload her yet. All work stopped in the dockyard. Every one was ordered to shelter for six hours. The

destroyer *Legion* received a devastating direct hit and
sank. Men struggled in the sea.

Then two large bombs whistled down towards the
two subs. One fell precisely between them, but its
shallow trajectory carried it through the water underneath P39. The bomb ploughed on and struck the wharf
wall violently, exploding as it did so. The water itself
seemed to detonate, and a cloud of spray surrounded the
sub. When it settled she had been split athwartships,
her back broken. Not a single casualty came from this,
as all the crew were sheltering. P39 was towed back to
Marsa and beached by the stern. Stores, spare gear, and
light machinery were taken to *Talbot*, but the submarine was subsequently hit repeatedly during April
and actually sank by the shore.

The other bomb of the two fell on the jetty alongside
Sokol and about fifty yards away, but it did not go off—
which was just as well, as it was a thousand-pounder.
Most of the attacks this day came from dive-bombers,
and altogether fifteen bombs fell in the creek where
Sokol lay.

March 27: Three heavy raids on Grand Harbour.
More of the convoy hit.

March 28: The inhabitants of Malta gave thanks at
their shrines for the weather being so bad that no air
attack developed all day. Simpson felt doubly relieved,
for a rare raid-free day meant repair work—on *Sokol*
included—and rest for the crews generally. Every one
was beginning to need it pretty desperately.

March 29: An air-raid warning awoke Lazaretto.
They heard it deep down in the Cavern—and groaned.
And Malta was under an alert the whole day. Single
planes came over every few minutes for twelve hours.

No work was done in the dockyard all day. The last raider left as the sun set.

March 30: All work on *Sokol* finished. She left Dockyard Creek for French Creek to be degaussed.

March 31: *Sokol's* degaussing done. The sub. was prepared for patrol. But heavy raids went on all day. Darkness. At 2000 hours forty bombers attacked Grand Harbour. The Greek submarine *Glavkos* and H.M.S. *Penelope* were lying in French Creek. *Sokol* was with them.

Then three one-ton bombs fell ten yards from *Sokol*, three tons of explosive radiating round 360 degrees. The result for *Sokol's* crew: ninety-eight cells smashed, many plates in the cells also broken, and the boat full of chlorine gas.

The Poles worked desperately in gas-masks all through the night. All damaged cells had to be disconnected before more fatal fumes spread—with no power, no dockyard labour, no telephone, no chance of getting a tug to shift the sub. But *Sokol* was not spent yet. Meanwhile, in the midst of the raid, the submarine *Pandora* arrived and made her way to Shell Pier, where she discharged white oils as more bombs burst.

April 1: *Sokol* staggered back to the dockyard to remove the damaged batteries. But heavy air attacks began again, and several bombs came close to her. The cruisers were leaving the anti-aircraft crews closed up for action, and all unnecessary ratings went ashore to shelter. The submarines in harbour became prominent among the day's targets—particularly *Pandora* and P36. *Pandora* moved over to Grand Harbour at dawn and secured to Hamilton Wharf in an effort to escape.

Simpson went down to see the sub. at 1030. He hurried over to her commanding officer.

"Think we'd better try and get you out of here to-day," Simpson said urgently. "If we can unload stores and torpedoes and refuel at the same time we'll shift you by 2200."

Simpson could see the danger.

An air-raid commenced as he was talking to *Pandora*'s commander and lasted six hours till tea-time. But, because of the extreme urgency of *Pandora* getting out of Malta with the least delay, it seemed justified to continue disembarking stores throughout the raid.

The first two hours of the alarm proved to be largely reconnaissance of the harbour areas. Then, between 1430 and 1500, a heavy raid of Junkers 88's followed by 87's developed on the harbour area. *Pandora* received two direct hits and sank in four minutes. Two officers and twenty-three ratings were killed. At the same second almost P36, alongside *Talbot*, was near-missed by a medium bomb, which fell three feet from the port forward end of the engine-room, and between the sub. and the Lazaretto building. The officers and two ratings aboard ascertained that the control-room after-bulkhead had been fractured, and then they abandoned her successfully. Luckily there was no loss of life.

A three-and-a-half-inch wire was at once passed round the conning-tower to hold the sub. upright, and to keep it to the building. But the wire parted before anything stronger could be got, and P36 rolled over into fifty feet of water and was lost.

"That's eight—including *Pandora*," Shrimp Simpson said sadly to Tanner. *Pandora*, of course, was not one of the flotilla, but they felt the loss as if she were.

But the day was not done. Simultaneously again, two or three sticks of bombs were flung north and south across Lazaretto Creek. *Unbeaten* lay submerged, but with the top of her conning-tower just awash. They near-missed her. The damage: distortion to the torpedo tubes, which led to the sub. being sailed for Gibraltar on April 9.

After the loss of *Pandora*, P36, and P39 it became all too apparent that any submarine visible to the enemy ran a strong risk of being sunk. Even *Unbeaten* had not been safe. Against this, it seemed to Simpson that the raiders could hardly expect to sink, damage, or even hit a submarine lying actually on the bottom in reasonably deep water. He could not consider probable yet that they would think it worth while to bomb open water in the harbour more or less on the off-chance of striking a sub.—though this is exactly what did happen later in April.

Things had got so bad by the beginning of April, how-ever, that Simpson called a conference of his heads of departments and the commanding officers of all sub-marines not out on patrol—and few were by now. It was a grimly determined, if rather gloomy, group that sat around in the dusty 'open-work' of the newly occupied wardroom.

"Gentlemen," Simpson started, "I've asked you all here to have your views on what we ought to do next. I know what I think, and I'll try and tell you how we stand. But I'm more than willing to discuss the position from every possible point of view before coming to any decision. First of all, we know that those longed-for Spit-fires will soon be here. Not to-day or to-morrow, but cer-tainly some time this month."

There were murmurs of approval.

"I know you are all nearing the end of your tether. You

can't go on for ever with this nightmare pattern of patrols and air-raids. But I want you to know the full facts. If we withdraw the subs. from Malta it means virtually stopping all offensive operations against Rommel's supply line. That's just what he wants most of all. The air offensive from the island is now practically non-existent—through no fault of the R.A.F. or Fleet Air Arm. And, another thing, the 10th Flotilla is the only remaining means of preventing the enemy from bombarding Malta by surface forces. Lastly, and perhaps most important of all, think what effect it would have on the garrison and local morale if they saw the flotilla fade away. With hardly any aircraft, ammunition and food running low, and little enough hope of relief that they can see, what will they feel if the flotilla saw no future in it? The Maltese might not, either. So I think we must stick it a little longer, somehow. Even a few weeks can make a lot of difference in the state of the war."

When he had received the obvious agreement of all in the room Simpson went on to outline the first of two plans. The idea was that the crews should temporarily lose their identity with particular submarines. And, to provide rest, each sub. should have a second crew from one of the others too badly damaged to operate efficiently. These two sets of crews would run alternate patrols. It was only since all but two of the subs. were identical that such a scheme had been mooted: and because of the urgency.

Naturally, no one was enthusiastic, but they were willing to give it a trial. However, they said they would be prepared to struggle on somehow as they were rather than adopt it. So after further discussion on detail Simpson unfolded the modified scheme he had up his sleeve in case they felt like that.

The crews of P36, P39, and a third crew, constituted from *Pandora's* survivors and spare officers, were to look after the subs. while they remained in harbour—the patrol crews getting away to rest-camps in the country. The subs. would still stay submerged by day. Patrols would have to be reduced in duration, and only four or five nights spent in harbour by the sub. between them. But by now, anyway, many preferred the peace of patrol to the bomb-battered rest available this April on Malta.

Simpson reported to Vice-Admiral, Malta, accordingly, and the proposals were forwarded to the C.-in-C., Mediterranean. Simpson would rather have seen his subs. and crews safely off the island, but the maintenance of the fortress seemed paramount at present. Anyway, it was a decision which would have to be reviewed daily. Life became an existence from one minute to the next.

April 2: Submarine officers were sleeping ashore, away from Lazaretto, on lodging allowance—that quaint official phrase born so many miles away at Whitehall.

The relentless raids went on. The three blocks of flats in Sliema used by the crews of *Unbeaten*, P34, *Urge*, *Sokol*, and a few other individual officers were all demolished by direct hits—pure flukes, but still annoying, because more accommodation had to be found. Needless to say, the dockyard again came to a standstill.

April 3: More raids. Two Junkers screeched into a spiral, hit by ack-ack. They both dived to death into Grand Harbour. But more took their place. While the bombs fell Simpson called another conference in the dockyard, to discuss the chances of carrying out repairs under existing conditions. All that could be done daily was to remove ten cells of *Sokol's* shattered batteries. As a result, the batteries were taken out by the crew and a band of volunteers from Lazaretto and an army camp near by.

During this day no fewer than twenty double red warnings moaned over the island; but the men kept at it, unloading and repairing a number of damaged cells.

April 4: By noon the crew had got thirty-one cells out of *Sokol*, but during the afternoon the power failed in the dockyard, putting an end to work. Then the raids restarted.

A large bomb struck the last remaining fuel lighter at Hamilton Wharf—and sunk the Greek sub. *Glavkos,* which had been refitting extensively since November and was within a week of sailing for Alexandria. But she had not then reached a fit state to dive during a raid, so could not avoid the point-blank attack on her.

Sokol suffered too. Within twenty-four hours of completing her repairs another near-miss cracked a couple of dozen containers. From now on it was decided essential to shift her from the dockyard and camouflage her alongside the hull of the *Essex,* an 11,000-ton motorship lying in Bighi Creek. She slipped out of the dockyard area that night, the only sign a slight movement of the moonlight reflected in the water. She lay with her bows aground and covered by nets and other camouflage devices.

This same day the light cruiser *Penelope* and destroyers *Havock* and *Lance* were damaged. *Havock* had been in the epic action at Narvik, among Norway's frozen fiords. Now she was living another, in the fury of Malta under fire.

Simpson ordered all subs. which could conceivably do so to dive by day wherever they were—in harbour or out.

April 5: Things grew worse for *Sokol*. Work on her in daytime was impossible now, and only one night in four could it be continued due to power shortage. She could not dive to the shelter of the harbour bottom, and she seemed to have been spotted by the morning reconnaissance: the plane that always came.

After lunch bombs fell around *Essex*, which was hiding her, and Simpson decided on a new berth for the submarine to lie next day. Meanwhile he also agreed to having one battery taken out that night. *Sokol* was towed back to the dockyard for the purpose, and the other sixty-six cells in her No. 1 battery were removed in four and a half hours. The crew of P39 helped the Poles in this remarkable feat.

Thereafter she was moved each morning, just before light, to a fresh billet and concealed as well as she might be, to try to avoid being seen from the air. One day would be spent among a clutter of barges and lighters in the commercial harbour of Marsa; the next day hidden by the overhang of a listing supply-ship beached in the bay.

April 6: *Sokol* was surrounded by barges at Marsa Creek, and lay with her stern aground. But the German reccy plane saw her; and bombers plastered the creek. None of the barges were sunk. *Sokol* suffered no damage, for a change.

April 7: Submarines still came and went. Patrols were paramount. Army camouflage experts assisted in hiding *Sokol*. Three more heavy raids on Marsa Creek caused devastation to the buildings around the area.

More than 300 bombers took part in the raid. Wave after wave brought a deathly dark to the sky. They sank twelve barges in the creek—but still *Sokol* escaped.

In this early-April period submarines hidden at the bottom of Mersa Mersetto Harbour were being shaken by the odd bomb that blasted the creek or fell around Fort Manoel or *Talbot* establishment. So Simpson had another headache. He arranged bottoming berths outside the harbour in 120 feet and clear of the protective minefield. But this did not prove very satisfactory, since subs. could not be surfaced readily in the event of heavy enemy ships approaching. And, as the island was virtually devoid of air reconnaissance, it became more than ever essential for the subs. in harbour to be at short notice to leave.

These vessels fit for patrol now faced just one more hazard, too. The odd assortment of minesweepers based on Malta had been gradually whittled away until only one remained.

One sweeper to tackle all the mines laid around the approaches to the island and in the harbours themselves!

Willing as this lone ship was, she could not possibly guarantee a clear passage in and out of Malta. The enemy could easily mine around the coast at this time, so the risk was great. But the submarines survived.

April 8: Four saturation raids involved 300 planes and finished off nearly all the buildings still standing around Marsa Creek—300 planes versus a handful. All the barges in the creek sank, and the nearest bombs fell only four yards from *Sokol*. Yet again she was shaken and shattered and battered, with over 400 holes found in the casing and conning-tower, including small holes in the pressure-hull. *Sokol*'s crew were not hurt, but they saw that the hull leaked in several spots. The bombs also damaged water and air pipes. Fire from one of the nearest explosions singed all the camouflage off the outside. They repaired the water and air systems and No. 1 battery tank. The rest would take longer. Commander Karnicki began to wonder whether *Sokol* would ever be fit for sea again.

Meanwhile the new routine of sending subs. on patrol after a few clear nights worked well—just so long as the operational crews could enjoy some rest on the island. But by April 8 the Germans found the rest-camps the crews were using and machine-gunned them daily. Later they began to be bombed as well. Simpson saw that this routine could not continue beyond a couple of patrols with one five-day rest, but he hoped that the strong fighter reinforcement, due in a fortnight or less, would wrest local air superiority over the island and so gain some respite.

April 9: *Sokol* moved alongside *Essex* again and camouflaged herself afresh. The battery was not ready, but Commander Karnicki got the sub. fit for diving. There were raids again during the day. That night *Sokol* shifted in to the dockyard, and the crew, plus five officers and nine ratings from the sub. base, loaded sixty-six cells in No. 1 battery.

April 10: Back to *Essex* went *Sokol* at the first streaks from the east sky. Heavy raids on Grand Harbour and the dockyard meant no power available, so no chance to load the rest of the battery that night.

April 11: Heavier raids, to saturation point. And still no power.

April 12: The Luftwaffe now knew where *Sokol* was. They directed an attack actually on *Essex* and the sub.

N

Many bombs fell around the ship. A hit on *Essex* caused her to catch fire. But *Sokol* somehow was not marked. After dark she returned to the dockyard to have the battery finished. By dawn it was complete and connected up. *Sokol* dived into Bighi Bay.

April 13: *Sokol* lay doggo all day on the bottom. The crew crossed their fingers. After dark she stole back to Lazaretto to prepare for sea. She was tempting Fate, but it could not be avoided.

April 14: She lay on the bottom in Mersa Mersetto Harbour all day, and once more surfaced after dark to continue preparations.

As Simpson chatted to Karnicki of the present position the Pole shook his head, saying: "Before, it was a joke. Now, it is no longer funny."

April 15: *Sokol* certainly bore a charmed existence. This day she stayed dived, and after dark crept towards the dockyard. Her bifocal periscope had to be changed, and a perforation in the pressure-hull patched. The periscope defect did not come to light until a trial dive in Mersa Mersetto Harbour.

In the darkness and heavy sea *Sokol* fouled the boom defences with her starboard propeller. She bumped nastily on the locks for two hours before finally clearing the boom. She continued her trip to the dockyard to embark her periscope and patch up the propeller just damaged. Nothing could stop her now, the crew hoped. The periscope was swiftly switched. And, although *Sokol* was still quite unfit for operations, she had to go. If she stayed much longer she would surely be sunk. Her 'luck'—if it could be called that—would not hold. There was time yet for her to be hit.

April 16: *Sokol* surfaced at noon, and entered the

dockyard again to load provisions and make ready for sea. By the grace of God no raids interfered with the plan. So *Sokol* was ready at last, with a patched pressure-hull, only one propeller working, and over 200 splinter holes still in her casing. "Honourable scars," as Simpson described them to Commander Karnicki.

April 17: One month, thirty-one days, since *Sokol* came in from patrol and moved into the berth by Lazaretto.

Now, at 0600, *Sokol* sailed, at a slow crawl to Gibraltar. She reached the Rock fifteen days later, *en route* for England. She arrived safely for her rest and refit—never more needed nor better earned.

Sokol was safe, *Glavkos* sunk.

The 10th Submarine Flotilla stayed on—and hit back hard. No one worked harder than Sam MacGregor and his repair staff. The drill in April was for them to toil all night on maintenance or repairs to bomb damage so that the subs. could go back to sea. And regularly, almost every day, a sub. went out on patrol, and one came home.

It was with relief that the crews left the noise and the death of the island for the Mediterranean; but they returned to it with interest, astonished to see how much Lazaretto had changed in the interim and how little was left of their dwindling personal possessions ashore.

Clothes presented a problem both for officers and ratings. What was salvaged from Lazaretto got buried again in the ruins of the civilian shore billets. Malta could offer no replacements, so that many submariners with a natural pride in their uniform did not 'go ashore' when they could, because they looked so unservice-like.

No convoys could hope to get through in sufficient strength to do much for the island, yet small supplies of essentials still arrived fairly regularly. All visiting submarines from other flotillas in the Mediterranean came crammed with stores such as torpedoes, dried eggs, milk, vegetables, petrol for the R.A.F., and ammunition for the guns.

The two supreme stalwarts in this carrier service were the submarines *Clyde*, under Commander Ingram and then Lieutenant Brookes, and *Porpoise*, under Lieutenant-Commander Pizey and later Lieutenant Bennington. These two subs. had been adapted to carry stores and petrol, and their arrival was always awaited keenly. Petrol is a particularly dangerous cargo in a submarine, for the slightest leak inconveniences the crew and may leave a tell-tale 'oil-slick' for all to see on the surface. These subs. could only bring a fraction of what was wanted, but every drop helped to keep the few Hurricanes airborne for a little longer. And, since those Spitfires were almost on the horizon, every day counted.

The submarines were unloaded at night, no attention being paid to the regular raiders of the Italian Air Force, which whizzed over the island at high speed. The large submarines lay alongside the little wharf at Msida while the crews and stevedores worked frantically to clear them before the bombs of the day. For it was round-the-clock air attack with no let-up. Like the Malta subs., before just light they would slide astern and submerge safely in deep water—a weird world, but a safe one. While they were dived in the harbour they could hear no sirens, no 'raiders passed' signals, and it must have made the crews anxious when their peace was suddenly shattered by the ominous thud of bursting bombs.

At one stage the Germans guessed what was afoot, for while *Clyde* lay on the bottom a formation flew in low and laid sticks of bombs right down Msida Creek and up Pieta Creek—and criss-crossed the junction between them. But *Clyde* survived the shock.

As April passed the enemy had virtual supremacy in the air over Malta. Yet they must still have been irritated by the substantial successes of the few fighters left to defend the island. To try to neutralize these, Kesselring sent over large forces of fighters with the briefing, "Keep Malta's planes grounded or annihilate them in the air." Then, at a suitable moment, in were hurled hordes of Junkers 88's to bomb and blast with only the ack-ack guns to stop them. These ground defences were now running short of ammunition. The shells and bullets had to be conserved for mass formations flying to vital targets. The days of big barrages were over, and small or single flights had to be left alone altogether. It was galling for the gun-crews, who could only watch helplessly. Short-range weapons had to hold their fire unless or until absolutely sure of hitting the plane. They could no longer keep up a stream of fire to force diving aircraft into evasive action.

This was what the Germans wanted. Malta might be unsinkable, but they were going to do their worst to make it as untenable as possible. They knew supplies were short, and that they had the power to prevent many being brought. It was only a question of time, they thought, before the island fell.

Every primary target lay more or less in ruins. To attack the dockyard again would just stir up the rubble and waste bombs. Valletta, Sliema, Floriana, Gzira— and all showed scars deep and devastating. St George's

Barracks lay flattened by two violently vicious attacks. The barracks had been known and respected by the Italians throughout the War, without any official notification, as a non-military refuge for wives and families of serving personnel. But it was bombed by the Germans just the same.

Assaulted too was a large, well-marked military hospital, miles from anywhere out by St Paul's Bay. The rest-camp at Ghain Tuffheia was fair game too, until some of the submariners snatched up machine-guns as a measure of protection against the marauding Me 109's. These Messerschmitts made the most of the island's impotence. With our own fighters grounded and ammunition running short, half a dozen or so of these aircraft swooped around Malta machine-gunning wherever it was safe for them to do so. Some flew almost at sea-level, and by peppering the posts actually incited the coastal defence gunners to retaliate—and use precious ammunition.

At last the improbable occurred. The enemy's stupendous shipping losses convinced them—correctly—that the subs. still operated from Malta, although seldom located in Marsamxett Harbour to be seen from the air. But reconnaissance planes in the Mediterranean reported the submarines' movements to and from the island, and the Germans, guessing that the vessels were lying on the bottom all day, started systematically attacking the open water of the creeks with heavy bombs. It was an operation unique in warfare.

To counteract this latest move, Simpson ordered the subs. to the further inconvenience of proceeding before dawn to bottoming-berths outside the harbour and returning to Lazaretto after nightfall. But, as has been seen, the difficulties of this manœuvre in the Malta of April '42, and with reduced crews operating in the dark, had soon led to its being abandoned. For one good reason—it cut down drastically the vital time available for repair work.

This last move by the enemy looked like proving the breaking-point. But the flotilla's flag still flew from Lazaretto, if literally a little tattered. The submarines returned to lying on the bottom in harbour during the day and risking being bombed.

After *Unbeaten*'s escape when her conning-tower was near-missed as it stuck out of the water she was severely damaged while totally submerged; but somehow she was lifted up again and brought back to base.

Nowhere was safe—not even the sea-bed. Never before or since has a submarine flotilla had to sustain such treatment in harbour.

18

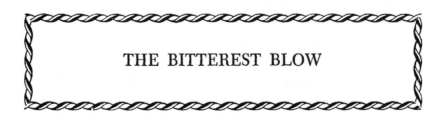

THE BITTEREST BLOW

In the midst of this mælstrom David Wanklyn took *Upholder* out of Malta on the morning of April 6 on his twenty-fifth patrol, the last she was due to do before returning to England.

After a successful rendezvous with *Unbeaten* west of Lampion Rock in the early hours of April 11 *Upholder* returned southward to patrol the western approach routes to Tripoli. Air reconnaissance later showed that an important convoy was approaching the port, so Simpson was ordered to assume operational control of all submarines in the Central Mediterranean to try to intercept it.

Shortly afterwards there were indications that two major merchant ships would be sailing at once to the westward, having discharged cargoes at Tripoli. Their probable route was estimated, and, since *Upholder* was on hand and had a short time to spare before making the rendezvous with other subs. on the patrol line, Wanklyn was told of the two ships' presence.

Since her speed of advance would not normally exceed two and a half knots during daylight and—allowing for charging—five knots between surfacing at 2030 and midnight, *Upholder* would have to dive at about 0530 on April 14 only fifty miles from the patrol-line position in order to be there by 0002 on the 15th.

Upholder was specifically sent by a route (through 33 deg. 25 min. N. and 13 deg. 40 min. E.) to keep her in deep water clear of mines, and also to allow *Urge* and *Upholder* to know their relative positions throughout the day. Assuming *Upholder* were safe at dawn on April 14, she would have dived about fifteen miles to westward of the position 33 deg. 25 min. N. and 13 deg. 40 min. E.—steering east.

Urge heard single depth-charges at fairly regular intervals on April 14, and at first this suggested the usual Italian practice of dropping one charge regularly while escorting a convoy. This may have been the case. If so, Wanklyn would have closed to attack, since a full outfit of eight torpedoes was assumed to be aboard. As noon approached *Urge* heard the depth-charging, hollow and heavier, and again in the afternoon. Sporadic charges crashed down till dusk.

Nothing more was ever heard of *Upholder*. After making twenty-five patrols and sinking an eighth of a million tons of shipping, Wanklyn went down.

It was feared that *Upholder* had finally been found by the enemy. The information office at Malta told Simpson that the Italian radio made a claim at 1300 and 1400 hours on April 18, quoting the name of the commanding officer of a torpedo-boat who had sunk a submarine in the Central Mediterranean.

Simpson sadly made his way to Combined Headquarters to report *Upholder's* loss to the Vice-Admiral. This was the bitterest blow of all borne by the flotilla.

Shrimp could still scarcely believe it. He had a hope somewhere that *Upholder* might be safe. He walked slowly. The wind whipped at his eyes, caught at his throat. Wanklyn had survived sixteen months. Now he would never know what it was like to bring *Upholder* back, proudly, peacefully, to Blockhouse.

On May 1 Mrs Wanklyn saw a large envelope stamped "On His Majesty's Service" lying on the mat. She slit it open. The single sheet was folded into three. She read:

> I am commanded by My Lords Commissioners of the Admiralty to inform you that the ship of which your husband, Lieutenant-Commander Malcolm David Wanklyn, V.C., D.S.O., Royal Navy, is in command is seriously overdue and considered to have been lost, and that your husband has accordingly been reported as missing. No details are at present available concerning the presumed loss of the vessel and some time may elapse before it becomes possible to come to a definite conclusion regarding your husband's fate.
>
> Meanwhile, My Lords desire me to express to you their very deep sympathy in the grave anxiety which this news must cause you, and to assure you that any further information that can be secured will be immediately forwarded to you.

The letter ended with the request that Mrs Wanklyn should not let any of the circumstances surrounding her husband's disappearance be known. The loss of *Upholder* was not to be announced at that stage.

With Wanklyn were lost: Lieutenant F. Ruck-Keene, R.N.; Sub-Lieutenant J. H. Norman, R.N.V.R.; Sub-Lieutenant P. R. H. Allen, R.N.; and a crew of twenty-eight.

"Tubby" Crawford had left some time earlier to take a commanding-officer's course, so survived.

At length the loss was made known. And after the formal text the Admiralty took the unusual step of adding a tribute to *Upholder*.

It is seldom proper for Their Lordships to draw distinction between different services rendered in the course of naval duty, but they take this opportunity of singling out those of H.M.S. *Upholder*, under the command of Lieutenant-Commander Wanklyn, for special mention. She was long employed against enemy communications in the Central Mediterranean, and she became noted for the uniformly high quality of her services in that arduous and dangerous duty. Such was the standard of skill and daring, that the ship and her officers and men became an inspiration not only to their own flotilla but to the fleet of which it was a part, and Malta, where for so long H.M.S. *Upholder* was based. The ship and her company are gone, but the example and the inspiration remain.

In the twenty-four successful patrols which this submarine had carried out in these waters she had built up a long record of success against the enemy, and of 36 attacks made, no fewer than 21 were successful. The *Upholder* sank:

    3 U-boats
    2 destroyers
    1 armed trawler
   15 enemy transports and supply-ships

But *Upholder* was gone. At the summer exhibition of the Royal Academy in 1943 David Wanklyn's portrait hung in honour. Officers of the submarine service had commissioned Harry Morley to paint it. The pose is against the top of the conning-tower, with the forward periscope up. Wanklyn's eyes are alight with anticipation. His hands hold a pair of field-glasses ready to scan the horizons. These were Wanklyn's goal, the far horizons of life, the unattainable.

One last letter—from Shrimp Simpson to Mrs Wanklyn:

What is it possible to write? Nothing that can in any way really help you, but perhaps some word from me may be acceptable.

You will remember me as David's captain in *Porpoise*, and throughout his brilliant career in the Mediterranean I have had the honour and the responsibility of being his Captain S.

It was largely for his safety that so little has been published to date of his outstanding successes—which number 21. As you must know from him he was shortly to have come home and reaped his hard won reward. I assure you that in his recent operations I have thought increasingly of his personal safety—thinking not only of him and you but of his great value to the country.

In February, I asked David if he would care to go home since I could arrange it, but very naturally his ambition was to bring *Upholder* safely back with him. I had little reason to suppose that this was tempting providence, he was so superbly confident. Furthermore, as my most able captain and devoted friend I was loath to part with him earlier than I had to. I only suggested it after feeling that his value was such that I disliked the attendant responsibility.

You will understand full well that David would not contemplate going home before his crew, who had served him with such bravery, devotion and success.

I have lost a friend and adviser whom I believe I knew better than my brother—to you I send all thoughts of sympathy in this terrible blow.

His record of brilliant leadership will never be equalled.

He was by his very qualities of modesty, ability, deter-
mination, courage and character—a giant among us.

The island of Malta worshipped him. This tribute is no
overstatement.

If I may ever help you please let me know. I shall
endeavour to meet you when I return someday, probably
after the war.

Yours very sincerely,
GEORGE SIMPSON
(known to David as Shrimp)

The ship with Wanklyn's personal possessions aboard
was sunk by the enemy. . . .

19

LUFTWAFFE VERSUS LAZARETTO

Was the flotilla finished at Malta? Simpson asked himself the question every day. Would it be better to withdraw and wage war from elsewhere? Against all the reasons for staying he had to weigh the safety of the subs. and the submariners. He would serve no purpose by staying only to see the flotilla sunk one by one in harbour and the crews either killed or left without ships to man.

By the time *Sokol* sailed and *Upholder* was lost the strain had got more severe—despite the success of the subs. on patrol. Simpson knew they were fighting a losing battle at Lazaretto when he told Tanner on April 19: "We've got to go on till the twenty-first, Geoff. The day after to-morrow. I've just heard. That's the date set for the Spits. I wonder if any aircraft have ever been so eagerly awaited anywhere before?"

It was generally assumed that as soon as the Spitfires got going they would lash the Luftwaffe and bring back peace over the island. Nothing could express eloquently enough the feeling of those few in Malta who knew that the fighters were on their way. Perhaps it was wishful thinking that they believed their troubles would be all over. Under a siege like the March–April onslaught perspectives became blurred. The Spitfires seemed a symbol of relief from it all. For had not the Few done wonders over the skies of Southern England less than two years earlier? Surely it would be repeated.

Effervescent excitement greeted the great day of April 21, 1942. The news was secret, but had spread to all the island. Every one gloated at the prospect of what was coming to the Germans. Then the aircraft arrived. Hopes in hundreds of hearts were pinned to these planes as their pointed wings dipped down and they landed between raids.

The immediate effect, as far as the submariners were concerned, was that air attacks became diverted during the next two days to the aerodromes.

Then came the breaking of the dream. By April 23, within forty-eight hours of touching down, the Spitfires had been reduced to less than a handful. It was too much to expect them to cope with the Luftwaffe in full force and fury—and still overwhelming odds.

The Germans had won the second round, and the situation deteriorated dramatically. It was soon realized that there would be no respite, no relief, no peace by day or night.

On the 23rd Simpson decided that the time had come for him to visit the Vice-Admiral again, and recommend that the flotilla would be forced to leave the island. Conditions had not improved one iota since the 21st; enemy minelaying was expected on some scale and there was nothing to combat; and the crews showed signs of deep fatigue, which it would be dangerous to ignore. For a refreshed crew was an essential, not a luxury, if the submarine war were to be

conducted with continued success. So the decisive die
was cast. He hated doing it, but he had to.

Simpson put the plan into operation to evacuate the
submarines and base staff. He decided to leave a
skeleton staff of two officers and the Maltese ratings to
continue improving the rock shelters. They also had
orders to do all they could to clear up the mangled mess
of Lazaretto for when the flotilla should be able to
return in better days: for return it would, he never
doubted.

Captain Simpson remarked in his report on this final
phase that "it naturally passed through my mind from
time to time during these last four months how much
pleasanter life would be if the submarine tunnels proposed in 1934 had been available"; a masterly understatement, and remarkably reticent for the man who had
to endure all the physical nightmare and also bear the
brunt of the responsibility for a flotilla at sea and in
harbour—never safe for a second.

During the 1930's many trials were conducted and
schemes submitted by farsighted officers who realized,
even in peace-time, what war with Italy would entail in
aerial activity against Malta. But money was short, and
the Admiralty could not see, even after the Abyssinian
affair, that the cost of carving such tunnels for the subs.
would have paid dividends out of all proportion to the
finances involved—for they would have allowed operations to be continued indefinitely against the enemy.
The price of the proposed submarine shelter tunnels,
completely bomb-proof, would have been equal to one
large sub. If only one less had been built half a dozen
U-class submarines could have continued at Malta, safe
against even a block-buster. £300,000 the Admiralty

saved—but they lost Lazaretto, or at least lost it as a serviceable sub. base.

The time to leave drew near. The intensity of the air assault had left some of the submarines so damaged by near-misses that they were unfit for operations without repairs; and repairs that the dockyard could not possibly undertake. These cripples were patched up as best they could be, and one by one they proceeded westward to Gibraltar—and so home for a refit.

The remaining five, *Urge*, *Una*, P31, P34, and P35, Simpson deemed fit to operate from elsewhere after reasonable repairs and a period of proper rest. So this quintet, bloody but unbowed, were filled to overflowing with spare crew, spare gear, and any personal kit that still survived, and they prepared to sail east to Alexandria.

Then the day after the decision to go, April 24, while P34 lay in deep water off the Valletta terminus of the Mersa Mersetto ferry, she was narrowly missed by a large bomb. She was waiting for nightfall to surface and prepare for sea, and, although on the bottom, was severely shaken.

Harrison, her commanding officer, and half the crew were aboard, and when they started to surface about 2030, just after dark, they found it very hard. They managed to manœuvre her astern to clear a supposed obstruction on the bows, but in so doing she got caught in an anti-torpedo net strung underwater across the harbour. Harrison blew her tanks, and she came up just so far—and stopped. She came to rest firmly and obstinately with a four-and-a-half-inch steel-wire hawser bar taut across the casing abaft the conning-tower.

After communicating by asdic and ascertaining her

o

position by smoke-candle Sam MacGregor brought his mind to bear on the problem. He arrived on the scene standing up in a skiff and brandishing a hacksaw. No one ever knew if he had filled in the requisite forms for this tool, but possession was ten-tenths of the law now. And, anyway, every order-book was burned on the island! Sam set to work parting the large, many-stranded steel wire under the strain of an awkward angle. One by one he sawed through the stout strands. After an hour the last few parted with a mighty twang—and P34 shot up to her full buoyancy. Sam returned to other business.

The raids of the 24th indicated that the enemy were still searching Mersa Mersetto Harbour specifically for subs., since many sticks fell in the water there. So, while the last five made final preparations to move to Alexandria, and in view of the waxing moon, subs. bottomed outside the harbour once more to be on the safe side. No other incidents occurred.

So ended the first phase of the 10th Submarine Flotilla's operations. The flotilla was constituted for the first time in naval history—after eight months as Malta Force Submarines—and by May 1, 1942, it had become a legend.

Although the operational difficulties were always immense, and increased by lack of electric light, telephones, and other amenities—such as the general mess dining-hall demolished on April 6—the enemy only won on land, and then only temporarily.

Under the water the flotilla sank in those last four months when everything was against them one 6-inch cruiser, one U-boat, two schooners, one salvage ship, and a trawler; and they blew up an Italian goods train.

Furthermore, they sank or damaged 60,000 tons of enemy supply-ships, all at a time when a thousand air-raids battered Malta in four months. And 10,000 tons of bombs were being dropped on target areas of the island. Manoel Island got some 400 hits. The period of alert averaged more than twelve hours out of each twenty-four.

Before Simpson and his staff left the island by plane to continue the fight from a better base he made sure that the essentials remained for operating the flotilla at Malta again, although just now it was dispersed, damaged, and had suffered such losses.

At the base of Lazaretto were mess-decks, repair shops, a periscope shop in the open, with store-rooms, offices, and sleeping space under rock. Workshops were being built underneath the rock too as he left. In the dockyard the battery-shed and electrical repair shops could be reconditioned in time. No. 1 dock was quickly repairable; and two cranes in the dockyard creek were still working. Once the raids ceased the subs. could carry on where they had to stop.

Simpson took a nostalgic last look at Lazaretto before joining Tanner in the battered car, which whisked them off towards the airfield. Through the open door of one of the workshops he glimpsed the Maltese shrine still intact after all the island had suffered.

The five submarines headed for Alexandria, leaving Malta with a strange mixture of relief and regret, just as they had done when going out on a patrol after the raids. They had all been through too much not to feel this moment deeply.

Una, P31, P34, and P35 arrived at Alexandria, but *Urge* was never heard of again after diving in departure

from the island. The loss of *Urge*, and her great commander, Tomkinson, was almost unbearable. First
Wanklyn, now Tommo had been killed: the two ack-
nowledged masters whose names had already echoed
round the wide waters of the Mediterranean. Even
though the very best submarine commanders were at
work in other Mediterranean flotillas, these two had no
superiors. The price paid by the 10th Flotilla for its
fame was high.

Ten submarines were lost in this sixteen months' saga.
Half of the total strength. *Upholder* was lost on her
twenty-fifth patrol; *Urge* on her twentieth.

From January 1, 1941, to May 1, 1942, fifteen submarines of the 10th Flotilla sank seventy-five enemy
vessels: 4 cruisers, 5 destroyers, 6 submarines, 6 transports, 39 supply-ships, 6 tankers, 1 A.M.C., and lastly
8 miscellaneous vessels.

75 ships with a total tonnage of nearly 400,000.

20

THE SIGNAL OF SUCCESS

THE sequel to the story is short. It came after another sixteen months had passed. During 1942 the Germans were diverted to the Eastern Front, and the war went well in Africa. The remnants of the 10th Submarine Flotilla, rested and repaired, returned to Malta before the raising of the siege. They were fortified by new sub. arrivals from Britain—in many cases commanded by previous first lieutenants of the original flotilla. They waged war relentlessly on the enemy's traffic in a style supremely worthy of Wanklyn and his men—so much so that Captain Simpson received the rare distinction, for a naval officer, of being mentioned in military despatches "for services rendered to the Eighth Army."

Few of the first band remained to see the enemy driven out of Africa and the triumphant assault on Europe from the south, culminating in the surrender of the Italian fleet. But those who were not at Malta in 1943, to witness what they had striven for during the darker years, had the satisfaction of reading Sir Andrew Cunningham's classic signal to the Admiralty on September 11, 1943:

> *From*: C. IN C. MEDITERRANEAN   *To*: ADMIRALTY
>
> Be pleased to inform their Lordships that
> the Italian battlefleet now lies at anchor
> under the guns of the fortress of Malta.

APPENDIX I

List of Submarines and their Commanding Officers which formed Malta Force Submarines and 10th *Submarine Flotilla*

(Decorations marked * were awarded for services rendered during the period covered by this book.)

UPRIGHT: Lieutenant E. D. Norman, D.S.O.,* D.S.C.
        Lieutenant J. S. Wraith, D.S.C.
UTMOST: Lieutenant-Commander R. D. Cayley, D.S.O.*
UNIQUE: Lieutenant A. F. Collett, D.S.C.*
UPHOLDER: Lieutenant-Commander M. D. Wanklyn, V.C.,* D.S.O.* (two bars posthumously).
USK: Lieutenant P. R. Ward.
        Lieutenant G. P. Darling.
URSULA: Lieutenant A. J. MacKenzie.
        Lieutenant A. R. Hezlet, D.S.C.*
UNDAUNTED: Lieutenant J. L. Livesay.
UNBEATEN: Lieutenant E. A. Woodward, D.S.O.*
UNION: Lieutenant R. F. Galloway.
URGE: Lieutenant-Commander E. P. Tomkinson, D.S.O.* and bar.
P33: Lieutenant R. D. Whiteway-Wilkinson, D.S.C.
P32: Lieutenant D. A. B. Abdy.
SOKOL: Commander Karnicki, V.M.,* D.S.O.*

P34: Lieutenant P. R. H. Harrison, D.S.O.,* D.S.C.
P31: Lieutenant J. B. de B. Kershaw, D.S.O.*
UNA: Lieutenant D. S. R. Martin.
       Lieutenant C. P. Norman.
P38: Lieutenant R. J. Hemmingway, D.S.C.
P35: Lieutenant S. L. C. Maydon.
P36: Lieutenant H. N. Edmonds, D.S.C.
P39: Lieutenant N. Marriott, D.S.C.
Spare Commanding Officer: Lieutenant J. D. Martin.

HEADQUARTERS STAFF

Captain G. W. G. Simpson, C.B., C.B.E.
Commander G. Tanner, O.B.E.
Lieutenant-Commander (E.) S. A. MacGregor, O.B.E.
Lieutenant-Commander R. Giddings, O.B.E.

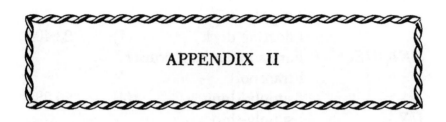

APPENDIX II

List of Successes achieved by Submarines during the Period covered

(Tonnage is expressed in Gross Registered Tons, and the list does not include ships damaged but not sunk, nor any gun or other actions against targets ashore.)

UPHOLDER:	2 destroyers		
	3 submarines		
	3 transports		
	10 supply-ships		
	2 tankers		
	1 trawler	(21)	128,353 tons
URGE:	2 cruisers		
	1 destroyer		
	1 transport		
	5 supply-ships		
	2 tankers	(11)	74,669
UTMOST:	1 transport		
	6 supply-ships	(7)	43,993
UNBEATEN:	2 submarines		
	2 supply-ships		
	1 tanker		
	1 collier		
	2 schooners	(8)	30,616

UPRIGHT:	1 cruiser		
	1 destroyer		
	4 supply-ships		
	1 floating dock	(7)	23,408
UNIQUE:	1 armed merchant cruiser		
	1 transport		
	2 supply-ships	(4)	20,382
UNA:	1 supply-ship		
	1 tanker		
	1 schooner	(3)	15,355
URSULA:	2 supply-ships	(2)	14,640
P31:	1 cruiser		
	1 supply-ship	(2)	12,100
SOKOL:	1 destroyer		
	2 supply-ships		
	1 schooner	(4)	7,642
P33:	1 supply-ship		6,600
P35:	1 supply-ship		
	1 salvage-tug	(2)	4,471
P38:	1 supply-ship		4,170
UNION:	1 supply-ship		2,800
P34:	1 submarine		1,461

Grand total ...   390,660